1972

TRISTAN TZARA

Dada and Surrational Theorist

Frontispiece: *Tristan Tzara*, Robert Delaunay, n.d. (charcoal sketch). Courtesy Mme. Sonia Delaunay. Photo Marc Vaux, Paris.

TRISTAN
TZARA

Dada and Surrational Theorist

By Elmer Peterson

RUTGERS UNIVERSITY PRESS
New Brunswick, New Jersey

Grateful acknowledgment for the use of copyright material is made to the following:

To Penguin Books, Ltd., for a poem from *The Penguin Book of French Verse,* translated by Anthony Hartley.

For a passage from *The Banquet Years* by Roger Shattuck, reprinted by permission of Joan Daves, copyright © 1955, 1957, 1958, 1968 by Roger Shattuck, published by Harcourt, Brace & World.

To Christophe Tzara for extracts from "Essai sur la Situation de la Poésie," "Initiés et Précurseurs," and *Inquisitions.*

To Editions Jean-Jacques Pauvert for extracts from *Sept Manifestes et Lampisteries.*

To Le Club Français du Livre for extracts from *Amours Jaunes* by Tristan Corbière.

For extracts from *Grains et Issues* and *Midi Gagnes,* copyright © by Editions Denoël-Paris.

To Doubleday & Company, Inc., for poems from *Alcools,* translated by William Meredith.

To Editions Gallimard for extracts from *Les Pas Perdus* by André Breton, *Oeuvres Complètes de Guillaume Apollinaire* (Biblio. Pléiade), and *Point du Jour* by André Breton.

To Editions Seghers for extracts from the series, Poètes d'Aujour-d'hui.

To Editions d'Art Albert Skira for extracts from *Picasso,* 1948.

FOR JUDITH, KRISTIN, AND ERIC

Acknowledgments

I would like to thank M. Christophe Tzara for permission to consult and quote unpublished material by his father; M. Michel Sanouillet for his reassurance and advice; Mme. Andrée Kail for her wise and patient help; The Colorado College for providing a generous research grant; my colleague Marcelle Rabbin for her help; M. François Chapon, Conservateur at the Bibliothèque Littéraire Jacques Doucet; Mme. Sonia Delaunay; Mr. Arturo Schwartz; and Mr. and Mrs. Leonard M. Brown.

E.P.

The Colorado College
Colorado Springs, Colorado
October, 1970

Contents

List of Illustrations

Introduction

« TOUT EST DADA »

Odéon Theatre graffito, May 1968

In some respects, 1968 might be considered the culminat-
ing dada year of the century. Throughout France, young
people violently and often poetically voiced their displeas-
ure with "the system." Opposition to a world formed by
their elders was expressed in graffiti all over Parisian walls:
"Papa stinks"; "If all the old people went hand in hand—
it would be ridiculous"; "Culture is the inversion of life";
"Young people make love, the old make obscene gestures";
"Under the paving stones—the BEACH."

In New York City, well-dressed patrons attending the
Museum of Modern Art *vernissage* of an exhibition called
"Dada, Surrealism, and Their Heritage" were heckled by

demonstrators who shouted, "Bourgeois slobs," and "Go to Schraffts!" These young "purists" objected that surrealism and dada were being defused of their revolutionary content. Some claimed that canons of good taste had guided the selection for the show. *The Great Masturbator* was included, but Duchamp's urinal was not. Certainly this object could have been reproduced when the exhibition reached the Art Institute in Chicago, for it was rumored that plumbing changes required by Dali's *Rainy Taxi* had knocked out an entire men's room.

Protest against this important exhibition took many forms. A "Chicago surrealist group" attacked, calling for a "vast, multi-level, interconnected program of CULTURAL GUERRILLA WARFARE." [1] In the same city, the Gallery Bugs Bunny prepared a poster calling the exhibition a "reprehensible fraud." Presumably resisting the Elmer Fudds of the art world, Bugs Bunny representatives spent Saturdays distributing leaflets outside the Art Institute. One member attended the first lecture of the show with a squawking horn. "Whenever the guy said something inaccurate or untrue, I honked. I must have honked it 500 times in 10 minutes." [2]

A confirmed dadaist might also have viewed the Democratic National Convention of 1968 as the supreme dada event of the year—a spectacularly large-scale production of Alfred Jarry's *King Ubu*. The list of characters in this play, which was a favorite of dadaists and surrealists alike, includes Palotins, conspirators and soldiers, a crowd, nobles, magistrates, counsellors, peasants, the Whole Russian Army, the Whole Polish Army, the Phynancial Horse, and The Disembraining Machine.

But perhaps we should go back some ten years to see how dada's influence has been steadily building. Early in the Spring of 1960, a bizarre and complicated machine created by Jean Tinguely did a jerky dance of death in the courtyard of New York's MOMA.[3] To the amusement of the onlookers, this assemblage of bicycle wheels, a toy wagon, an old piano, and other junk performed a rite of auto-destruction which had important implications in the realm of art and thought in general. In a similar vein, some poets discarded the elegy in favor of the "howl" and accompanied their poetry readings with insults hurled at the audience, adding an occasional public disrobing for emphasis.[4]

Such demonstrations have their roots in the dada spirit, a spirit which, instead of perishing when the Parisian Beaux-Arts students dumped the coffin of dada in the Seine one day in the early twenties, seems to be more than ever with us today.

The significance of Jean Tinguely's *Homage to New York* has been described by John Canaday who said that "for the dadaist, including the current crop of neo-dadaists in the flourishing revival, despair may be assuaged by the act of negative creation, the creation of objects that offend others by denying hope, that shock them and thus affirm the personality of the despairer."[5] Despair and excessive

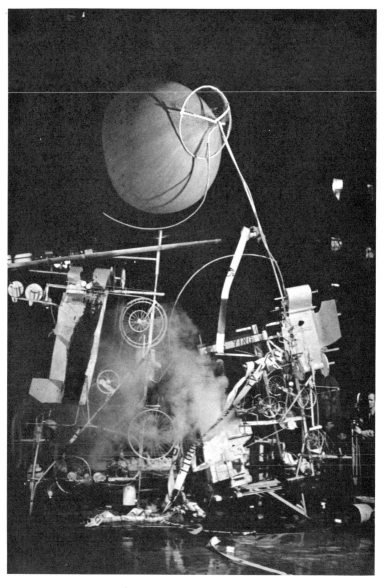

Figure 1. Hommage à New York, Jean Tinguely, 1960 (self-destroying sculpture). Photo by David Gahr; © copyright 1970.

self-affirmation were surely two of the main traits of dada. The systematic belittlement of art, as illustrated by a work which destroys itself or, in another case, a painting whose colors run completely off the canvas—to the delight of the artist if not the owner,[6] is a cornerstone of dada which continues to be important today.

The mere title of the poem "Howl" is also significant from the dada point of view. Convinced of the inadequacy of language, the dadaists made their own kind of poetry out of a shout or a curse. Another important facet of dadaism which has been revived is the *blague*. The dadaists elevated the spoof to the rank of a dogma. The fact that an American publishing house, Grove Press, devoted an entire issue, No. 13, of its *Evergreen Review* to "What is Pataphysics?" demonstrates that the spoof as an answer to the tragic events of the day is very much alive.

The documents of the original dada movement are still in circulation, delighting some and consternating many. A dada retrospective in West Germany [7] had an "unparalleled success." This exhibition seemed to strike a responsive chord in a country where "the economic miracle" had in many cases put things before ideals and discipline before fantasy. Another illustration of dada's presence was the frantic bidding produced at Kornfeld and Klipstein's in Berne on 12 June 1968, when some three hundred items from Tristan Tzara's library were put up at auction.

A number of books on the subject of dada have appeared during the last ten years. One of the first and still one of

the most helpful for an understanding of the movement
is *The Dada Painters and Poets*[8] by Robert Motherwell.
Besides being the most inclusive anthology of the writings
of dada, it is also replete with photographic reproductions
of many pamphlets by members of the movement. This
important book also contains a fine critical bibliography,
compiled by Bernard Karpel, Librarian of the Museum of
Modern Art in New York.

One of the original dadaists, Marcel Janco, has assisted
Willy Verkauf in an important essay, *Dada, Monograph of
a Movement*.[9] Georges Hugnet has published *L'Aventure
Dada*,[10] a history of the movement, and Gabrielle Buffet-
Picabia, Francis Picabia's widow, has compiled a study[11]
which is especially helpful in understanding dada's origins.
Another original dadaist, Georges Ribemont-Dessaignes,
has written *Déjà Jadis ou du mouvement Dada à l'espace
abstrait*,[12] and Raoul Hausmann, *Courrier Dada*.[13] Among
the more recent works, mention should be made of Richard
Huelsenbeck's *Dada*[14] and the brilliant *Dada à Paris*[15] by
the President of the Association for the Study of Dada and
Surrealism, Michel Sanouillet. This association cooperated
in a Symposium on Dada and Surrealism, sponsored by the
Graduate Division of the City University of New York
and held in late March, 1968.

All this activity points up the fact that the dada spirit
is alive and well today. The world is once again, as it was
in 1916, thrust into a climate of doubt and hopelessness.
Moreover, the inability to comprehend the fast-moving

and menacing discoveries in science give rise to a feeling of perplexity and uncertainty which finds its artistic expression in dada.

The parallel success of dada in West Germany and in the United States must also be explained. Perhaps it is a protest against the empty boasts of the "economic miracle" and the "great society." Reacting violently to the insipid, the predictable, the mechanical, the dadaist has always refused to accept half truths. He combats smugness by the unexpected and by pure chance. A good example of this is Marcel Duchamp's *Why not sneeze?* This work consists of a bird cage apparently filled with sugar cubes. Upon picking up the cage, however, one is astonished by its weight; the cubes are actually made of marble. This is a dada reply to smugness and a dada denial of sweetness.

Why not sneeze? requires the public's participation, just as dada theatre and its current offspring, the Happening, do. Describing the first dada soirée, Henri Béhar states, "In this way, then, the organizers [Tristan Tzara *et al.*] arrived at their goals, to make the public react, to make it demonstrate, finally through an iconoclastic verve, through noise, insults, shouts, sounds, and meaningless gestures, to cretinize it totally, to make it lose all notion of the Good and the Beautiful." [16] Frequently the audience at a Happening is drawn directly into the action; at the very least it must react creatively, making some sense out of the action. The first "dada visit and excursion" (held on April 14, 1920), which was to launch a series of visits "especially to chosen

Figure 2. Why not Sneeze Rose Selavy?, Marcel Duchamp, 1921 (ready-made). Courtesy Philadelphia Museum of Art, Louise and Walter Arensberg Collection. Photo A. L. Wyatt.

spots which really have no reason to exist" has a modern counterpart in Happenings like *City Scale,* in which the audience traveled around New York City in two trucks. The original dadaists would also have approved the chosen locations for performance of Claes Oldenburg's *Washes* and Dick Higgins' *The Tart*—the first in Al Roon's pool in the basement of New York City's Riverside Plaza Hotel, and the latter in New York's Sunnyside Gardens boxing ring.

The self-destroying machine by Tinguely, the "howl" of the beat poets, the resurgence of pataphysics, and the current general influence of dada demonstrate a modern crisis of the mind. Coupled with this crisis of the mind is an acute linguistic crisis. At a time when communication seems so important, many artists are suggesting that it has never been so difficult and unsatisfactory. The impassioned harangue of Lucky in Samuel Beckett's *Waiting for Godot* is typical of this crisis.

> . . . and considering what is more that as a result of the labors left unfinished crowned by the Acacacacademy of Anthropopopometry of Essy-in-Possy of Testew and Cunard it is established beyond all doubt all other doubt than that which clings to the labors of men . . . it is established beyond all doubt that in view of the labors of Fartov and Belcher left unfinished for reasons unknown. . . .[17]

This torrent of nonsense underlines a modern breakdown in communication. The word has become impotent, and this impotency is nowhere made more clear than in the writings of the dadaists. The passage from Beckett and the endless clichés of Mr. and Mrs. Smith in Ionesco's *Bald Soprano* are but two of the best known examples of a crisis of language of which Jean-Paul Sartre says: "Whatever have been the social and historical factors, it [the crisis of language] manifests itself by attacks of depersonalization of the writer vis-à-vis words." [18] The dadaists and surrealists expressed this depersonalization constantly, dadaists affirming the impotency of words used in traditional contexts, and surrealists insisting on the promise of a new verbal promiscuity. As André Breton said: "Words, moreover, have quit playing around. Words are now making love." [19]

The following study will consider the significance of Tristan Tzara in relation to the modern crisis of mind and idiom. He has been for some time a curiously neglected figure. Possible reasons for this neglect are the repeated efforts of André Breton to minimize his, and dada's, importance, the fact that he was a foreigner, and the attempts by some critics to slight a man who for most of his life was a Marxist.

Tzara, however, is difficult to leave without discussion as it was his dynamism and vision that made dada a force throughout the world after the First World War. "Reformed" dadaists such as Breton and Richard Huelsenbeck have contradicted Tzara's claim to inventing dada,[20] and they have disagreed with his methods, but they were forced to acknowledge the influence of this slight and myopic man who from Zurich in 1916 began roaring out with a clamorous voice against traditional morality and traditional aesthetics. This young Rumanian reached out to artists in many other countries, uniting them in a new and strident opposition to traditionalism. Their common disenchantment with all the manifestations of bourgeois culture was complete. They were to create a new art more in keeping with the irrationality of the times, and Tristan Tzara was to be their chief press agent.

Tzara went to Paris in 1919 after a long correspondence with Paul Dermée,[21] Francis Picabia, André Breton, Louis Aragon, and Philippe Soupault. He was awaited, as Breton says, "a little like the Messiah."[22] Soupault describes his activity:

> A few weeks after his arrival, he exploded. He deployed a tremendous activity. His hotel, to the great terror of the manager, became a sort of headquarters. Tzara had become an impresario, magazine director, ticket seller, publicity chief, typographer, editor, organist. . . .[23]

This human dynamo finally turned to surrealism in the late twenties, contributing to *La Révolution Surréaliste*,[24] and to *Le Surréalisme au Service de la Révolution*.[25] In the mid-thirties he formally became a Marxist, and he remained a Marxist until his death in 1963.

In brief this is the man: father of dada and a surrealist who left this group for more strictly political action.

Figure 3. Une Nuit d'Echecs Gras, Tristan Tzara (publicity flyer). Reproduced from Michel Sanouillet, *Francis Picabia et 391,* vol. 1, p. 92 (Paris: Eric Losfeld, 1966).

He prefaced nearly a dozen books by modern writers and
painters and wrote a score of articles on others. In addition,
two substantial volumes, on Rabelais and Villon, were left
unpublished at his death. He composed some three dozen
volumes of poetry and five plays. But despite this pro-
digious career he is singularly neglected. The only substantial criticism of his poetry appears in the excellent
introduction by René Lacôte to *Tristan Tzara* in the
Poètes d'Aujourd'hui series,[26] and in the perceptive chapter
on Tzara in *The Poetry of Dada and Surrealism* by
Mary Ann Caws.[27] There is a brief but interesting introduction to Tzara's work by Jean Cassou in *Tristan
Tzara, Morceaux Choisis*.[28] At this writing no book-
length critical study on Tzara has appeared, and there
have been surprisingly few references to his theoretical
work, yet it is this theoretical work which became
more and more important to him in his latter years. Among
the mass (the word is used advisedly, there being for
example some six thousand letters) of material left by
Tzara and now at the Bibliothèque Littéraire Jacques
Doucet in Paris are his projects for a three-volume edition
of his critical essays. The first volume of this work, the
Pauvert edition of the *sept manifestes DADA, lampisteries,*
was completed. Two companion volumes were contem-
plated, one tentatively entitled *Mémoires sur l'art de voir
et de toucher (Statements on the Art of Seeing and Touching)* or *Le Pouvoir des images (The Power of Images).*
This book would include his art criticism, from the articles

on Precolumbian and African art to his studies of modern painters such as Picasso, Max Ernst, and Joan Miró. The projected third volume, which he called *Les écluses de la poésie* (*The Floodgates of Poetry*), would include the theoretical articles written in the thirties on poetry, a section on certain poets such as "Les Bousingots," François Villon, Tristan Corbière, and Arthur Rimbaud, and a final section on modern writers, among them Guillaume Apollinaire, Pierre Reverdy, Raymond Radiguet, Antonin Artaud, and Nazim Hikmet.

The Doucet collection also contains additional evidence of Tzara's importance as an interpreter of literary and artistic movements. An example is the text of his radio addresses delivered in Paris in 1950 on *Les Revues de l'Avant-Garde*. In these nine programs, Tzara, who knew his subject as well as anyone could, having contributed to all or nearly all of these magazines and having edited two of them, discussed *Les Soirées de Paris; Maintenant* and *Sic; Nord-Sud; Dada; Littérature; Proverbe, 391, Cannibale; Le Cœur à Barbe, Littérature* new series; and *La Révolution Surréaliste*. He also left a plan for a study of revolutionary spirit in French poetry.

It is hoped that some day Tzara's projects will be realized and that his collected works will appear, demonstrating Tzara's importance as poet, dramatist, and theoretician. Two key works to an understanding of the theoretical category will certainly be the manuscript on François Villon, which, although announced for publication by

Fasquelle in Paris for early 1960, was not published and is not as yet available for consultation at the Doucet, and the volume on Rabelais, which is also not yet available. Tzara's two-volume *Secret of François Villon* was the result of some four years of hard work in his rue de Lille apartment, in the same building where the poet Lautréamont had once lived. Surrounded by books, papers, paintings by his dadaist and surrealist friends, and pieces of African and Oceanic art, the father of dada worked patiently to discover hidden meanings in Villon, whose *Testament* has been called the "birth certificate of modern poetry." The man who is all too frequently dismissed as a destroyer of language, a dadaist literary terrorist, had become in fact a serious literary scholar. He was also a brilliantly perceptive admirer of things as diverse as African art (witness the invitation to him in 1962 to participate in the Congress of African Culture in Salisbury, Rhodesia) and Romanesque churches of Catalonia which Georges Sadoul claimed he knew better than anyone. This extraordinary man was equally at ease in a technical conversation about the work of Nils Bohr or the theories of Heisenberg. It is not surprising that his son is an eminent French scientist.

Tzara's lifelong effort seems to have been to understand and to interpret the evolution of art and its relationship with society. In this effort he turned back to Villon and to Rabelais. After patient effort, he believed that he had found a series of complicated anagrams which unlocked the secret intentions of Villon, bringing fresh light to events in the poet's life and providing us with proof that certain poetic work, attributed to another, was actually by Villon. The same painstaking deciphering of anagrams in Rabelais resulted in other important discoveries having to do with the chronology of Rabelais' life and work, and the attribution of another work to the father of *Gargantua*. The importance of these studies will have to be assessed by experts, but their importance to Tzara himself cannot be denied. He spent the last days of his life painfully moving to his desk to work on the Rabelais manuscript and finally signaling from under an oxygen tent corrections to be made in the text. In time the results of this passion for understanding and interpreting Rabelais and Villon will be judged, and in time there will surely be books on Tzara, the poet. This study takes fully into account the pitfalls mentioned by Louis Aragon who said: "The commentators have the floor from now on, and God knows what they'll want to make of this man whose tie they'll have trouble straightening. They'll have even more trouble in reducing to order this great disorder which he put into words." [29] The intent of this book will not be to straighten ties or to adjust Tzara's critical monocle, but to present him as an important avant-garde theorist and to trace chronologically his seminal contribution to the interpretation of modern aesthetics.

« ICI ON SPONTANE »

University of Paris,
Censier graffito, May 1968

PART ONE

Dada

1 Dada Manifestoes and Early Celestial Adventures

messieurs mesdames achetez entrez achetez et ne lisez pas vous verrez celui qui a dans ses mains la clef du niagara l'homme qui boite dans une boîte les hémisphères dans une valise le nez enfermé dans un lampion chinois vous verrez vous verrez vous verrez la danse du ventre dans le saloon de massachussets [*sic*] . . .[1]

[messieurs mesdames buy come in buy and don't read you'll see the man who holds in his hands the key to niagara the man who stalls in a stall the hemispheres in a valise his nose wrapped in a Chinese lantern you'll see you'll see you'll see a belly dance in the massachussets saloon . . .]

The barker is Tristan Tzara, the circus, dada. The remainder of Tzara's spiel for this three-ring literary circus is expressed in his *sept manifestes DADA,* which present the least misleading, if not always the clearest, definition of the aims of the dada movement.

Before studying these manifestoes and the play, *La Première Aventure céleste de M. Antipyrine*, from which the first manifesto is taken, we might present Tzara's credentials as chief barker for dada. Others who were important in shaping dada theories and attitudes include Richard Huelsenbeck, whose association with dada dates from its beginnings to the present day.[2] Mr. Huelsenbeck, however, is primarily associated with German dadaism, a politically oriented movement that was in opposition to the original nonpolitical ideals set forth in the Zurich proclamations.

What of André Breton? The periodical, *Littérature*, of which Breton was an editor, heralded dadaism, and for nearly five years he was closely identified with the movement in Paris. Breton, however, did less for dada than Tristan Tzara. Its activities suited his temperament less, and Breton's personal testimony and that of his friends Louis Aragon and Philippe Soupault clearly show that it was Tzara's energy, imagination, and courage which accounted for the success of dada in Paris. The monumental and indispensable *Dada à Paris*[3] contains unpublished letters from Breton in Paris to Tzara in Zurich which show the kind of awe in which Tzara was held by his French admirers and the eagerness with which his arrival in Paris was awaited. Breton's letter of January 22, 1919, is an example.

Your manifesto fired me with enthusiasm; I no longer knew from whom I could expect the courage which you demonstrate. All my attention is turned toward you today. (You don't really know who I am. I'm twenty-two. I believe in the genius of Rimbaud, Lautréamont, Jarry; I loved Guillaume Apollinaire exceedingly, I feel a profound tenderness for Reverdy. My favorite painters are Ingres and Derain; I am very impressed by Chirico's art.) I am not as naïve as I seem.

Others, besides me, follow you with confidence; I have spoken at length about you with Braque, Derain, Gris, Reverdy, Soupault, Aragon.

. . . Aren't we going to see you in Paris soon? [4]

But Breton's initial fervor for the movement and for its Zurich leader eventually waned, and five years later he could write:

Although Dada had, as they say, its moment of glory, it is not greatly mourned: in the long run its omnipotence and its tyranny had made it unbearable.[5]

Quoting Francis Picabia, Breton asserts: "You have to be a nomad, passing through ideas as you pass through countries or cities." [6] It is because of this nomadic bent that Georges Ribemont-Dessaignes called Breton "Andréas the chameleon." Breton's temperament was unsuited to prolonged dadaist activities, for he found it impossible to tolerate dadaism's chaotic individualism and its negative orientation. It is significant that while the dada manifestoes are usually individual efforts, the surrealist pronouncements are often signed collectively. Furthermore, Breton's order to abandon dada:

> Leave everything. Leave Dada. Leave your wife. Leave your mistress. Leave your hopes and your fears. Leave if need be a comfortable life. . . . Take to the roads.[7]

is followed almost immediately by:

> Picabia, Duchamp, Picasso are still with us. I shake hands with you, Louis Aragon, Paul Eluard, Philippe Soupault, my dear friends forever. Do you remember Guillaume Apollinaire and Pierre Reverdy? Isn't it true that we owe some of our strength to them? And already Jacques Baron, Robert Desnos, Max Morise, Roger Vitrac, Pierre de Massot await us.[8]

We have the vision of Breton courageously setting off on the roads of new aesthetic adventure—flanked by a rather large group of kindred souls. Further evidence that Breton was a reluctant dadaist after a year or two of involvement in the movement following Tzara's arrival in Paris, is given by his (Breton's) abortive attempt in 1922 to establish a Congrès de Paris, with the aim of giving a more *positive* orientation to avant-garde art. Any single orientation at all was totally contrary to the spirit of dada. For these reasons, then, André Breton's identification with

Figure 4. Tristan Tzara, Robert Delaunay, 1923 (oil on cardboard, 105 x 75 cm.). Courtesy Mme. Sonia Delaunay. Photo Marc Vaux, Paris.

dada must be considered less complete and sincere than Tristan Tzara's. For an insight into the dada movement, whose limits I shall quite arbitrarily fix from 14 July 1916—the date of Tzara's first dada play—to 6 July 1923 —the night when the dadaists, gathered for Tzara's third play, *Le Cœur à Gaz,* had a wild free-for-all among themselves—there is no better guide than the writings of Tristan Tzara.

The first major dada work is Tzara's *Première Aventure céleste de M. Antipyrine.*[9] This short play had its initial performance at Waag Hall, Zurich, on 14 July 1916. It seems appropriate that it was performed on Bastille Day, for in a sense it marks an assault on the bastion of aesthetics. *The First Celestial Adventure* grew out of the atmosphere of Zurich's Cabaret Voltaire, the meeting place for the dadaists. These young men, most of them expatriates, were united in their aversion to what they considered a senseless war and in their rejection of the traditional concept of art. One of them, Hugo Ball, in his *Flight from Time* said: "It is necessary to define the activity of this cabaret; its aim is to remind the world that there are independent men beyond war and nationalism—who live for other ideals." [10]

The title, *La Première Aventure céleste de M. Antipyrine,* gives an indication of the play's style. Although it has been translated as the *First Celestial Adventure of Mr. Fire-Extinguisher,* it seems that it would be proper to substitute Aspirin for Fire-Extinguisher, as Antipyrine was a popular headache remedy at the time in France and Switzerland. Tzara, frequently troubled by severe headaches, was probably familiar with the product. Nevertheless, either choice may have validity. Antipyrine could be the man able to snuff out the flames of an odious war, or he could be the one to cure humanity of the headache caused by (to borrow an existentialist expression) bad faith and bad art. Marcel Janco, the Rumanian painter and dadaist, was in charge of the sets for the play, a simple job, since, as he says: ". . . all our sketches were of an improvised nature, full of fantasy, freshness, and the unexpected. Thus there were few costumes, little direction, and few sets." [11]

The advertisement for *La Première Aventure* is a typical dada brag: "Impotence cured prepaid on request." Perhaps one can interpret this as something more than a joke, as Tzara decided that his mission was to cure a certain kind of literary impotency and to restore magic power to *words*. Indeed, he would later attempt to cure mental impotency, making poetry *a state of mind*. Tzara wished to restore magic power to the word by assembling oddly disparate words in poems to create a verbal equivalent of the collage technique used by dadaist artists like Kurt Schwitters, who would pick up odds and ends in the street for his works. Some of the gratuitous wordplay Tzara delighted in may in part be explained by the fact that, although well schooled in French, he did not learn French as his native language. French words had a curious resonance for him, and he felt no restraint at all in using them in new and unexpected ways.

Let us examine in some detail the verbal techniques which make *La Première Aventure* so unusual. One is first struck by the names of the characters: Mr. BleuBleu, Mr. CriCri, La Femme Enceinte (the pregnant woman), Pipi, and Mr. Antipyrine. Infantile names like BleuBleu, Cri-Cri, and Pipi have a contemporary progeny in Samuel Beckett's Gogo and Didi in *Waiting for Godot*. Indeed there are several instances in which contemporary dramatists, notably Beckett and Ionesco, employ dadaist techniques. This is confirmed by Richard Huelsenbeck. "The heritage of Dada as far as the stage is concerned was materialized only today and is felt mostly in the works of Ionesco." [12] Rosette Lamont also agrees with this view.

> . . . Ionesco and Beckett, a Rumanian and an Irishman writing in French (not the sonorous language of classicism, not the decorous tongue of diplomats, but a primitive, transparent language, drained of its vital juices, strangely and marvelously atonal, a language used not for communication but to produce sounds made to re-echo in the void), have gone even further in their exploration of despair, the sickness of the void which the existentialists called "nausea." [13]

This description of the language of Beckett and Ionesco could also be applied to the language of dada as it is first expressed in *La Première Aventure céleste de M. Anti-*

pyrine. Tzara's is obviously "a language used not for communication," at least not for normal modes of communication, with the Zurich audience in 1916. Dialogues such as the following illustrate the point.

La Femme Enceinte:

Toundi-a-voua
Soco Bgai Affahou.

Mr. BleuBleu:

Farafangama Soco Bgai Affahou.[14]

Several passages in African—and pseudo-African—tongues reveal two things; that Tzara was not interested in communicating something intelligible to his Swiss audience, and that he was interested in Africa. His expression, like Beckett's and Ionesco's, is used to "produce sounds made to re-echo in the void," the emphasis being on the sound rather than the meaning.[15] Tzara playfully repeats last syllables or groups of syllables.

dodododo
immense panse pense et pense pense
Erdera Vendrell [16]
endran drandre
rendre prendre entre rendre rendre prendre prendre

This is pure "sonorous inanity" but with a purpose, the purpose being to point up the hollowness of words and to confirm the belief that rational communication is often absolutely impossible. It is also abundantly clear that the language of dada is "not the decorous tongue of diplomats."

l'organe sexuel est carré est de plomb est plus gros que le volcan et s'envole audessus [sic] de Mgabati

le grand nommé BleuBleu grimpe dans son désespoir et y chie ses manifestations

oiseaux enceints qui font caca sur le bourgeois

[the sexual organ is square leaden bigger than the volcano and flys off over Mgabati]

[the tall one named BlueBlue climbs up in his despair and from there shits forth his demonstrations]

[pregnant birds which crap on the bourgeois]

The language of dada as expressed by Tzara is a faithful mirror of the cruelty and inhumanity present in a world gripped by war. He mentions patching up stomachs, split heads with mustard pouring out, and despair and calamity in general. One of his characters moves ". . . avec l'empressement d'un enfant qui se tue." [with the alacrity of a child killing itself.] This cruelty is reminiscent of that found in the poetry of Lautréamont, which Tzara appreciated as much as did Breton.[17]

Along with the meaningless repetition of certain sounds, Tzara uses the parallel device of enumeration. This repeated use of long lists of unrelated objects becomes another dada technique to block any communication of rational meaning.

Quatre cents chevaux soixante chameaux trois
cents peaux de zibelines cinq cents peaux d'hermines
son mari est malade
vingt peaux de renard jaunes trois peaux de chelizun
cents peaux de renard blancs et jaunes
un grand oiseau en vie Tyao
ty a o ty a o ty a o
et quatre beaux fusils [18]

[four hundred horses sixty camels three hundred sable skins five hundred ermine skins her husband is sick twenty yellow fox skins three chelizun skins a hundred white and yellow fox skins a large and living Tyao bird ty a o, etc. and four lovely guns]

This kind of enumeration has also been employed, although much later, by other poets, notably Jacques Prévert. It can be used to convey the weight of inanimate things on the earth, the existentialist idea of *contingence,* and the dull repetition of human experience.

Verbal collage has been mentioned, and Tzara brings this about by juxtaposing totally unrelated words, thus permitting a fresh vision of the world. The normal sentence structure is completely discarded in favor of free new associations of words.

> je pousse usine dans le cirque Pskow
> [I push factory in the Pskow circus]

> maisons flûte usines tête rasée
> [houses flute factories shaved head]

> la fièvre puerpérale dentelles et SO_2H_4
> [puerperal fever lace and SO_4H_4]

> Farafangama les mollusques Pedro Ximinez de Batnmar
> gonflent les coussins des ciseaux Ca_2O_4SPh
> [Farafangama the molluscs Pedro Ximinez de Batnmar
> puff up the pillows of the scissors Ca_2O_4SPh]

It must be pointed out that although juxtaposition was not an invention of the dadaists, it nevertheless was one of their favorite techniques. Among the most important innovators who showed the way for Tzara in this respect was Guillaume Apollinaire. A good example of his use of juxtaposition is the poem "Lundi Rue Christine."

> Ces crêpes étaient exquises
> La fontaine coule
> Robe noire comme ses ongles
> C'est complètement impossible
> Voici monsieur
> La bague en malachite
> Le sol est semé de sciure

Alors c'est vrai
La serveuse rousse a été enlevée par un libraire [19]

[These pancakes were exquisite
The fountain flows
Black dress like her nails
It's totally impossible
Here you are, sir
The malachite ring
The ground is strewn with sawdust
Then it's true
The red-headed waitress was carried off by a librarian]

Rather than a simple enumeration of unrelated *things*, this is an example of the juxtaposition of unrelated fragments of different conversations. It is a technique which had a great attraction for Tzara, as it sabotaged logical semantic order and progression of thought. The abruptness and scrambled quality of the expression was thought to have validity in that it captured the sometimes haphazard train of thought.

The dada use of simultaneousness is closely connected with this technique of juxtaposition and has been brilliantly studied by Roger Shattuck in his *Banquet Years*.

Ultimately it becomes apparent that the mutually conflicting elements of montage (or collage)—be it movie or poem or painting—are to be conceived not successively but *simultaneously*, to converge in our minds as contemporaneous

events. . . . The aspiration of simultanism is to grasp the
moment in its total significance or, more ambitiously, to
manufacture a moment which surpasses our usual perception of time and space.[20]

Tristan Tzara is one of the most diligent practitioners of
"simultanism" in letters. *The First Celestial Adventure*
furnishes two excellent examples of his use of this technique.

MR CRICRI	zdranga zdranga zdranga zdranga
MR BLEUBLEU	di di di di di di di di
PIPI	zoumbaï zoumbaï zoumbaï zoumbaï
MR ANTIPYRINE	dzi dzi dzi dzi

MR CRICRI	crocrocrocrocrocrodril
LA FEMME ENCEINTE	crocrocrocrocrocrocrodrel
PIPI	crocrocrocrocrocrocrocrodrel
MR ANTIPYRINE	crocrocrocrocrocrocrocrocrodral

Although this is simply an exercise in simultaneousness of
sound, Tzara did write simultaneous poems in which
some meaning is conveyed.[21]

These then are the principles and techniques expressed
in *La Première Aventure céleste*. They seem to be ani-
mated by a double desire to irritate and to mystify. The
indelicacies and the combative tone of the play were cal-
culated to enrage a certain spectator or reader: the
bourgeois. The mystification comes about through the

resolutely anti-communicative nature of the lines. Meaning is destroyed in several ways, the most obvious being the use of Africanesque mumbo jumbo. The playful treatment of words through the abandonment of logic in favor of alliteration also contributes to this breakdown of meaning, as does enumeration, which may simply be a whimsical game or may perhaps have a deeper significance. Tzara may have sensed that this method could show the brute existence of *things* devoid of meaning. Perhaps he saw as did Sartre's Roquentin that: ". . . there was no half-way house between non-existence and this flaunting abundance. If you existed, you had to *exist all the way,* as far as mouldiness, bloatedness, obscenity were concerned." [22]

Turning from this early and significant expression of the techniques of dada, let us now discuss further dada *theory* as set forth in Tristan Tzara's *sept manifestes DADA.* [23] These manifestoes contain the most important and complete discussion of the aims of Zurich-Paris dada by an original dadaist during the movement. They span a period of four years, beginning with the first, which was an integral part of *La Première Aventure,* to the last two, which were read in December of 1920.

The first manifesto, commonly called *Le Manifeste de M. Antipyrine,* was read by Tzara himself at the July 14, 1916, performance of *La Première Aventure.* There are three main ideas expressed in this short manifesto. They are the assertion that dada is not a literary school, that dada is decidedly against the war, and finally that dada is irrevocably opposed to traditionalism in literature. Linked with the first declaration, that dada itself is not just another literary school, is the admission that it is not in itself of the slightest importance. Tzara says modestly: "Dada est notre intensité: qui érige les baïonnettes sans conséquence. . . ." [24] The bayonets are fixed menacingly, but, significantly, the attack is inconsequential. In a clearer if less delicate statement Tzara asserts: "DADA reste dans le cadre européen des faiblesses, c'est tout de même de la merde . . ." [25] [Dada remains within the European framework of weaknesses, it's shit after all.]

In *Le Manifeste de M. Antipyrine,* Tzara makes his position clear with respect to Marinetti's futurist movement. He did not want dada to be identified with this group as it had been in the review *Sic,* which printed Marinetti and Tzara almost side by side. "Dada est l'art sans pantoufles ni parallèles; qui est contre et pour l'unité et décidément *contre le futur* [my italics]. . . . [26] [Dada is art with neither slippers nor parallels; it is against and for unity and is decidedly against the future. . . .]

Tzara also expresses horror at the insanity which permitted the war. He looked down on the collective lunacy from his "balcony" of dada, which might of course mean not only from a lofty intellectual noncommitment, but also from the heights of neutral Switzerland. One thinks in this respect of Romain Rolland's *Au-Dessus de la Mêlée.* Tzara describes his vantage point as

. . . le balcon de Dada. . . . D'où l'on peut entendre les marches militaires et descendre en tranchant l'air comme un séraphin dans un bain populaire, pour pisser et comprendre la parabole.[27]

[Dada's balcony . . . from where you can hear the military marches and come swooping down, slicing the air like a Seraph in a public bath, to piss and to understand the parable. (parabola?)]

The parable is too difficult to decipher, the rather basic gesture being simply one of supreme disgust. Tzara, who was just twenty at this time, seemed particularly fond of this means of expressing his contempt for humanity. "Il n'y a pas d'humanité il y a les réverbères et les chiens." [28] [There is no humanity there are streetlamps and dogs.] Like the Seraph relieving himself in the public bath, the dog has to content himself with a rather ineffectual gesture of opposition to the streetlamp—establishment. Influenced perhaps by the dada example, Richard Schechner, editor of the New York *Drama Review*, led a similar protest recently at the Pentagon, describing the action as "an effort to convert a biological need into a symbolic physical demonstration." [29]

Robert Motherwell, the American painter and dada scholar, has called *Le Première Aventure* and its manifesto an action of protest against the First World War.[30] It should be added that it is also a strong attack on the accepted artistic theories of the time. I have mentioned how series of apparently unrelated words brought about total dislocation of meaning. Let us now, examining the *Manifesto of Mr. Antipyrine,* further describe literary techniques and attitudes which were behind this attack on rational communication.

> L'art était un jeu noisette, les enfants assemblaient les mots qui ont une sonnerie à la fin, puis ils pleuraient et criaient la strophe, et lui mettaient les bottines des poupées et la strophe devint reine pour mourir un peu et la reine devint baleine, les enfants couraient à perdre haleine.[81]

> [Art was a nutty game, children put words together that had a ringing at the end, then they shouted and cried out stanzas, putting dolls' boots on them and the stanza became a queen and died a little and the queen became a tureen, and the children ran all the way to Abilene.]

This sentence is typical of Tzara's dada statements in that it is both serious and absurd. The thought is dissolved once again by a playful alliteration. It is also a serious and provocative condemnation of the actual state of poetry. When Tzara says art is a game, he is decrying the uselessness of purely technical virtuosity, of cleverly assembling words with "une sonnerie à la fin." In this central statement of disaffection with the accepted type of poetry, Tzara claims that poetry making has become nothing more than a game. The doll's boots, the rigid rules of versification, have made the game complicated but puerile. The triumph of the formal exigencies of the stanza has ballooned so menacingly that one flees from writing verse. This entire sentence, which appears nonsensical on the surface, becomes, on closer inspection, a condemnation of the "cries and tears" and empty sonority which Tzara felt to be the stuff of most poetry. He did not believe that the old form of poetry conveyed meaning. If poetry was only an exercise in virtuosity and a feeble pastime, then the dadaist had every right to employ a sonorous mumbo jumbo—but without pretense—in his own work. Thus, this first manifesto is an important statement, which presents the dada movement as unimportant in itself but resolutely antitraditionalist in literature and dedicated to pacifism.

The second dada manifesto was the *Manifeste Dada 1918*. It was read in Zurich at the Meise Hall on 23 March 1918, and appeared the same year in *Dada 3*. A much longer and more complete exposition of the dada position, it had an important effect on some of the more important avant-garde figures in Paris and was called "a decisive proclamation" by André Breton.[32] In the first section of the manifesto, God makes one of his rare appearances in Tzara's works. "Son existence fut déjà prouvée par l'accordéon, le paysage et la parole douce." [33] [His existence was already proved by the accordion, the landscape, and the dulcet word.] Tzara places himself with the rebels who revile the concept of art as celebration. Indeed, in the second part of this manifesto, he attacks the very idea of a work of art.

> L'œuvre d'art ne doit pas être la beauté en elle-même, car elle est morte; ni gaie ni triste, ni claire ni obscure, réjouir ou maltraiter les individualités en leur servant les gâteaux des auréoles saintes. . . .[34]

> [A work of art must not be beauty in itself, for beauty is dead; nor should it be gay or sad, light or dark, to delight or mistreat the individual by serving him the pastries of saintly haloes.]

Tzara would always maintain that a work of art was only significant in relation to a certain moment in time. As early as 1918 he expresses this view of art as evolution which would later be confirmed and strengthened through his acceptance of the Marxist dialectic. It should be pointed out, however, that at no time during this early period in his career did he express any specific political opinions—aside from counseling noninvolvement. It seems most likely, despite certain later statements,[35] that he rejected all forms of political activity during the life of dada.

Tzara is just as categorical in his opposition to formal artistic schools.

> Nous avons assez des académies cubistes et futuristes: laboratoires des idées formelles. Fait-on l'art pour gagner de

l'argent et caresser les gentils bourgeois? Les rimes sonnent l'assonance des monnaies et l'inflexion glisse le long de la ligne du ventre de profil. Tous les groupements d'artistes ont abouti à cette banque en chevauchant sur diverses comètes. La porte ouverte aux possibilités de se vautrer dans les coussins et la nourriture.[36]

[We have had enough of cubist and futurist academies, those laboratories of formalist ideas. Is the goal of art to earn money and to fondle the nice bourgeois? Rhymes jingle the same sound as coins, and inflexions slide along the profile of the belly. Every group of artists has finally arrived, astride various comets, at the bank, the door opened to the possibility of wallowing in cushions and rich food.]

From this, one can see that he envisioned dada as a *prise de position,* a radical rejection of all accepted aesthetic values and artistic movements. The dadaists certainly owed much to the schools of cubism and futurism, but their chief theorist rejects both.

Le cubisme naquit de la simple façon de regarder l'objet: Cézanne peignait une tasse 20 centimètres plus bas que ses yeux, les cubistes la regardent d'en haut, d'autres compliquent l'apparence en faisant une section perpendiculaire et en l'arrangeant sagement à côté . . . Le futuriste voit la même tasse en mouvement, une succession d'objets l'un à côté de l'autre agrémentée malicieusement de quelques lignes-forces. Cela n'empêche que la toile soit une bonne ou mauvaise peinture destinée au placement des capitaux intellectuels.[37]

[Cubism arose from a particular way of looking at an object. Cézanne would paint a cup 20 centimeters beneath his eyes; the cubists look at it from above; and still others complicate its appearance by making a perpendicular section and placing it discreetly to the side. . . . The futurist sees the same cup in motion, a succession of objects one next to the other, and he mischievously adds some lines of force. This doesn't prevent the canvas from being either good or bad painting destined for the investment of intellectual capital.]

These two approaches, cubism and futurism, are too timid for Tzara, as he calls for an art form which is not in the normal sense of the word representational, one which will give no comfort through recognition.

Le peintre nouveau crée un monde, dont les éléments sont aussi les moyens, une œuvre sobre et définie, sans argument. L'artiste nouveau proteste: il ne peint plus (reproduction symbolique et illusionniste) mais crée directement en pierre, bois, fer, étain, des rocs, des organismes locomotives pouvant être tournés de tous les côtés par le vent limpide de la sensation momentanée. Toute œuvre picturale ou plastique est inutile; qu'elle soit un monstre qui fait peur aux esprits serviles, et non douceâtre pour orner les réfectoires des animaux en costumes humains, illustrations de cette triste fable de l'humanité.[38]

[The new painter creates a world whose elements are also its implements. It is a sober and well-defined work which presents no argument. The new artist protests. He no longer paints (symbolic and illusionist reproduction) but creates directly in stone, wood, iron, tin, rocks, locomotive organisms which can be turned in all directions by the limpid wind of momentary sensation. All pictorial or plastic art is useless; let it become a monster to terrorize servile spirits instead of a sugary decoration for the refectories of animals in human dress, illustrating that sad fable which is mankind.]

Tzara is explicit here in saying that the new painter does not copy from reality, but instead creates his own imaginary world. Thus he very early discerns a current of modern painting from Marcel Duchamp and Francis Picabia which continues through the surrealists to the abstract expressionists or to *l'art brut* of Jean Dubuffet, and which also has a literary counterpart.

Il y a une littérature qui n'arrive pas jusqu'à la masse vorace. Œuvre de créateurs, sortie d'une vraie nécessité de l'auteur, et pour lui. Connaissance d'une suprême égoïsme, où les lois s'étiolent. Chaque page doit exploser, soit par le sérieux profond et lourd, le tourbillon, le vertige, le nouveau, l'éternel, par la blague écrasante, par l'enthousiasme des principes ou par la façon d'être imprimée. Voilà un monde chancelant qui fuit, fiancé aux grelots de la gamme infernale, voilà de l'autre côté: des hommes nouveaux. Rudes, bondissants, chevaucheurs de hoquets. Voilà un monde mutilé et les médicastres littéraires en mal d'amélioration.[39]

[There is a literature which doesn't reach the voracious mass. It is the work of creators and issues from a real necessity of the author and for the author. It demonstrates the knowledge of a supreme egoism, where laws wilt. Each page must explode, either through a profound and heavy seriousness, the whirlwind, dizziness, the new, the eternal, through the humiliating hoax, through the enthusiasm of principles, or by the way the page is printed. Here is a tottering and fleeing world, engaged to the bells of the infernal scale. Here on the other hand are the new men, rude, pouncing, riders of hiccups. Here is a mutilated world with literary charlatans adrift in their efforts at improvement.]

One can find no better description of much of Tzara's own poetic creation than "Rudes, bondissants, chevaucheurs de hoquets." His poem "Maison Flake" is an example.

déclenchez clairons l'annonce vaste et hyaline
    / animaux du service maritime
forestier aérostatique tout ce qui existe chevauche
    / en galop de clarté la vie
l'ange a des hanches blanches (parapluie virilité) [40]

[launch bugles the vast and glassy announcement
    / animals of the maritime service
aerostatic forest ranger all that exists rides
    / in a gallop of brightness life
the angel has white hips (umbrella virility)]

This obviously is a new poetry created for the artist himself. Tzara will later modify this particular position under pressure of a socialist conviction, but his verse is at this time nonlogical and hermetic. "L'art est une chose privée, l'artiste le fait pour lui; une œuvre compréhensible est produit de journaliste. . . . "Il nous faut des œuvres fortes, droites, précises et à jamais incomprises." [41] [Art is a private affair, the artist does it for himself; an understandable work is a journalistic product. . . . We need works that are strong, straight, precise, and forever beyond understanding.]

With dadaist vigor, Tzara says: ". . . il n'y a pas de commencement et nous ne tremblons pas, nous ne sommes pas sentimentaux. Nous déchirons, vent furieux, le linge des nuages et des prières, et préparons le grand spectacle du désastre, l'incendie, la décomposition." [42] [There is no beginning and we do not tremble. We aren't sentimental. Like a furious wind we tear apart the linen of clouds and prayers, and we prepare the great spectacle of disaster, fire, and decomposition.] The artist becomes a sort of *kamikaze,* expressing what Professor Armand Hoog has called "une métaphysique de la perdition." "Que chaque homme crie: il y a un grand travail destructif, négatif à accomplir. Balayer, nettoyer." [43] [Let each man cry out: there is a great destructive and negative job to be done. Sweep out, mop up.] These proclamations make Tzara's intent clear, and they also point up some differences between the negations of dada and the affirmations of surrealism. Tzara's will to destruction does not seem to be confined to literature, for he calls on the poet to depict runaway worlds in collision and decomposition. It is ironic that such a nihilistic attitude has so much positive value as prophecy. Tzara's modern reworking of the Book of Revelation (considering the means of destruction available today) is perhaps an accurate description of a coming holocaust.

In this same *Manifeste Dada 1918,* read by its author in Zurich, one can discern a paralyzing nihilism which sometimes cripples Tzara's fierce revolutionary impulse. "Mesurée à l'échelle Eternité, toute action est vaine." [44] [Measured by the scale of eternity, all activity is vain.] This extreme dadaist nihilism would later end up in an inevitable cul-de-sac, and surrealism would come forward to give a more positive direction to some of the dada aspirations. It is noteworthy that although Tzara attacks art, he admits that it is the only possible way out in an absurd world.

> Mais si la vie est une mauvaise farce, sans but ni accouchement initial, et parce que nous croyons devoir nous tirer proprement, en chrysanthèmes lavés, de l'affaire, nous avons proclamé seule base d'entendement: l'art. Il n'a pas l'importance que nous, reîtres de l'esprit, lui prodiguons depuis des siècles. [45]

> [But even if life is a bad joke, with neither end nor initial labor, and because we think we should get out of it unsullied, as chrysanthemums washed clean of the affair, we have proclaimed art as the sole basis of understanding. It

doesn't have the importance that we, mercenaries of the mind, have claimed for it for centuries.]

Tzara wishes to strip away all the old concepts by installing the spontaneous as supreme principle. "DADA; croyance absolue indiscutable dans chaque dieu produit immédiat de la spontanéité . . ." [46] [DADA, absolute and incontestable belief in every god that is the immediate product of spontaneity.] This fervent belief in spontaneity was to outlive dada, becoming one of the cornerstones of the surrealist effort, the spontaneous or automatic being an integral part of Breton's definition of surrealism as "Pure psychic automatisme by which an attempt is made to express either verbally, in writing, or by any other manner the true function of thought." [47] Proof that Breton also was fascinated by the spontaneous is shown by the first of his two short dada manifestoes, written before 1924, when he says: "DADA, acknowledging only instinct, condemns explanation a priori. According to Dada, we must not retain any control over ourselves." [48]

Another statement from Tzara's important *Manifesto Dada 1918* shows that some of his attitudes are quite close to those held by André Gide. One thinks of *Les Nourritures Terrestres* when reading Tzara's assertion that "Tout produit du dégoût susceptible de devenir une négation de la famille est *dada;* protestation aux poings de tout son être en action destructive. . . ." [49] [Any product of disgust capable of becoming a negation of the family is dada; a protest with the clenched fist of its whole being in destructive action.] Although Gide's attitude toward dada and the dadaists was somewhat ambivalent, leading Francis Picabia to state that if you read Gide aloud long enough your breath would stink, some encouragement for the young movement can be found in Gide's article of April, 1920, in *La Nouvelle Revue Française* which analyzes the dadaist attack on language.

> Already the edifice of our language is too undermined for anyone to recommend that thought continue to take refuge in it. And before rebuilding it is essential to cast down what still seems solid, what makes a show of still standing. The words that the artifice of logic still lumps together must be separated, isolated. They must be forced to parade again before virgin eyes like the animals after the deluge, issuing one by one from the ark-dictionary, before any conjugation. And if, through some old and purely typographic convention, they are set end to end on a single line, take care to arrange them in a disorder in which they have no *reason* to follow one another—since, after all, it is at the antipoetic *reason* that you are railing.[50]

Tzara, in the 1918 manifesto, expresses the belief that dada's role transcends this literary debarkation. His definition of the function is broader than Gide's. "Dada; abolition de la mémoire: DADA; abolition de l'archéologie: DADA; abolition des prophètes: DADA; abolition du futur. . . ."[51] This desire for the abolition of everything that would bind men to history was repeated in a phrase ascribed to Descartes and emblazoned on the cover of *Dada 3*, saying "Je ne veux même pas savoir s'il y a eu des hommes avant moi." [I do not even wish to know if there have been other men before me.]

Dada is thus presented as a nihilistic attitude which accepts only the moment. It refuses to atone for the past or to delude itself by trusting in a happier future. This detachment from history naturally carried with it the setting loose of family ties [52] and indeed the rejection of all authority and tradition. The fact that this defiant attitude was not always followed to the letter by the dadaists is attested by Gide's description of a dada soirée:

> I attended a Dada meeting. It took place at the Salon des Indépendants. I hoped to have more fun and that the Dadas would take more abundant advantage of the public's artless amazement. A group of prim, formal, stiff young men climbed onto the stage and, in chorus, uttered insincere audacities. . . . From the back of the hall someone shouted: "What about gestures," and everyone laughed, for it was clear that, for fear of compromising themselves, none of them dared move a muscle.[53]

It was not Tzara's fault that they did not act; in the *Manifeste Dada 1918* he had incited to riot. In its attack on formalism in the arts, on artistic schools, on communication in general, and in its praise of the spontaneous, it is perhaps the most far-reaching and significant of all the dada manifestoes.

The third dada manifesto, *Proclamation sans prétention*, was to have been read at the eighth dada soirée, on 8 April 1919, at the Kaufleuten Hall in Zurich. It appeared in *Anthologie Dada,* and the reason for its not being read was described in Tzara's *Zurich Chronicle*: "Tzara prevented from reading the Dada Proclamation, delirium in the hall, voice in tatters drags across the candelabras, progressive savage madness twists laughter and audacity. . . . Dada has succeeded in establishing the circuit of absolute unconsciousness in the audience which forgot the frontiers of education of prejudices, experienced the commotion of the new." [54] The commotion at this soirée as in most dada soirées was caused by shouted manifestoes, short skits, simultaneous poems, and noise music made by banging on pots and pans. If the audience this particular night had permitted Tzara to read his proclamation, they would have been introduced to "l'anti-philosophie des acrobaties spontanées." [55] The prefix *anti* runs through his works from *Antipyrine* to *Antitête*, and *antiphilosophie*. The Tzara of the dada period is the anti-man who only later, as a surrealist, becomes the approximate man. Two of the anti-man's statements in this proclamation are: "Nous affirmons la VITALITE de chaque instant" and "Le talent QU'ON PEUT APPRENDRE fait du poète un droguiste AUJOURD'HUI. . . ." [56] [We affirm the vitality of each instant. The talent that can be learned makes today's poet a druggist. . . .] Poetry is obviously not a technique. It is instead a way of looking at things—a particularly disapproving way for the dadaist.

The fourth dada manifesto is *Le Manifeste de M. Aa l'Antiphilosophe*. It was read in Paris at the Grand Palais des Champs Elysées on 5 February 1920, and subsequently appeared in *Littérature*, no. 13. This very short manifesto presents nothing new or remarkable. It did give Tzara the opportunity to call his audience idiots several times, although he admits that "we are all idiots." The next manifesto was *Le Manifeste Tristan Tzara*. This short scatological and propagandist missile is included in the *Manifesto of Mr. Aa the Anti-Philosopher* in *The Dada Painters and Poets* but was published separately by Tzara in his *sept manifestes*. It was read at the Université Populaire in Paris on 19 February 1920. It also appeared in *Littérature*, no. 13. In it Tzara calls as much attention to himself as to the movement.

tristan tzara

Regardez-moi bien!
Je suis idiot, je suis un farceur, je suis un fumiste.
Regardez-moi bien!
Je suis laid, mon visage n'a pas d'expression, je suis petit.
Je suis comme vous tous! [57]

[Take a good look at me!
I'm an idiot, I'm a joker, I'm a fake.
Take a good look at me!

I'm ugly, my face has no expression, I'm small.
I'm like all of you!]

In an unnecessary footnote he adds "I wanted to give myself a little publicity." The audience which heard *Monsieur Aa nous envoie ce Manifeste* was invited at the end of the reading to "Slug yourself in the face and drop dead." [58] In the same manifesto Tzara finds a striking image which describes perfectly his treatment of ideas. "Dans la chevelure des notions je plante mes 60 doigts et secoue brutalement la draperie, les dents, les verrous des articulations." [59] [I plant my 60 fingers in the tresses of notions and brutally shake the drapery, the teeth, the bolts of the joints.]

In the next manifesto, *dada manifeste sur l'amour faible et l'amour amer,* [60] this violent mental agitation is most apparent. In this very important statement, Tzara elevates the spontaneous and the fortuitous to the rank of guiding principles. He expresses his belief in the spontaneous in the famous phrase: "La pensée se fait dans la bouche." [61] [Thought is made in the mouth.] If words had become bankrupt and absolutely meaningless, then those coming directly from the mouth would be as valid as those formed in the mind. "Mes chers confrères: bon mauvais, religion poésie, esprit scepticisme, définition définition, *voilà pourquoi vous crèverez tous.* [62] [Dear colleagues: good bad, religion poetry, mind scepticism, definition definition, that's why you'll all bite the dust.]

Certain words which once carried considerable weight had now lost all reliability and could be used in a fortuitous manner in dadaist poetry.

Pour Faire un poème dadaiste

Prenez un journal
Prenez des ciseaux
Choisissez dans ce journal un article ayant la longueur
que vous comptez donner à votre poème.
Découpez l'article.
Découpez ensuite avec soin chacun des mots qui forment
cet article et mettez-les dans un sac.
Agitez doucement.
Sortez ensuite chaque coupure l'une après l'autre.
Copiez consciencieusement
dans l'ordre où elles ont quitté le sac.
Le poème vous ressemblera.
Et vous voilà un écrivain infiniment original et d'une
sensibilité charmante, encore qu'incomprise
du vulgaire.[63]

[To Write a Dada Poem]

[Take a newspaper. Take some scissors. Pick out an article which is as long as you wish your poem to be. Cut out the article. Then cut out carefully each of the words in the article and put them in a bag. Shake gently. Then take out each piece one after the other. Copy them down conscientiously in the order in which they left the bag. The poem will resemble you and you will find yourself to be an infinitely original writer with a charming sensitivity even though you will not be understood by the vulgar.]

Professor Alfred G. Engstrom of the University of North Carolina has found two or three quite similar recipes for poetry, one of them (astonishingly enough) by Leconte de Lisle, who obviously was opposed to this way of composing verse.[64]

Tenez, prenez un chapeau, mettez-y des adverbes, des conjonctions, des prépositions, des substanifs, des adjectifs, tirez au hasard et écrivez; vous aurez du symbolisme, du décadentisme, et de l'instrumentisme et de tous les galimatias qui en dérivent. Vous riez? Mais je vous assure que c'est sérieux; ce qui'ils font n'est pas autre chose. Ce sont les amateurs du délire dont parle Baudelaire.[65]

[Look, take a hat and put in it some adverbs, conjunctions, prepositions, nouns, adjectives, pull out at random and write. You will have some symbolism, decadentism, instrumentism, and all the nonsense that comes from these. You laugh? But I assure you that it's serious; what they do is nothing else. They are the lovers of delirium whom Baudelaire speaks about.]

Professor Engstrom does not mention another significant "lover of delirium," who also makes a contribution in this respect. He is Lewis Carroll who, in *Poeta Fit, non Nascitur,* gives his own version of words in a hat.[66]

First learn to be spasmodic
A very simple rule.
For first you write a sentence,
And then you chop it small;
Then mix the bits, and sort them out
Just as they chance to fall;
The order of the phrases makes
No difference at all.

Then if you'd be impressive,
Remember what I say,
The abstract qualities begin
With capitals always:
The True, the Good, the Beautiful—
Those are the things that pay.[67]

Tzara knew perfectly well that "those were the things that pay," but he thought them meaningless and not worth selling. Indeed he found the whole *pose* of intelligence meaningless.

L'intelligent est devenu un type complet normal. Ce qui nous manque, ce qui présente de l'intérêt, ce qui est rare parce qu'il a les anomalies d'un être précieux, la fraîcheur et la liberté des grands antihommes, c'est

L'IDIOT

Dada travaille avec toutes ses forces à l'instauration de l'idiot partout.[68]

[The intelligent man has become the complete and normal type. What we need, what offers some interest, what is rare because it has the anomalies of a precious being and the freshness and freedom of great antimen, is the IDIOT. Dada is working with all its forces toward the establishment of the idiot everywhere.]

He defines the activities of the idiot's organization:

DADA est un microbe vierge
Dada est contre la vie chère
Dada
société anonyme pour l'exploitation des idées
Dada a 391 attitudes et couleurs différentes suivant
le sexe du président
Il se transforme—affirme—dit en même temps
le contraire—sans importance—crie—pêche
à la ligne.
Dada est le caméléon du changement rapide et
intéressé.
Dada est contre le futur. Dada est mort. Dada est idiot.
Vive Dada. Dada n'est pas une école littéraire, hurle

Tristan Tzara[69]

[DADA is a virgin microbe
Dada is against the high cost of living
Dada
limited-liability company for the exploitation of ideas
Dada has 391 attitudes and different colors according to
the president's sex

It changes itself—affirms—says at the same time
the opposite—no matter—shrieks—goes fishing.
Dada is the chameleon of quick and selfish change.
Dada is against the future. Dada is dead. Dada is idiotic.
Long live Dada. Dada isn't a literary school, shouts

Tristan Tzara]

The dada attitude is one of complete indifference, and the choice between shrieking and going fishing is absolutely insignificant. As for the number of different dadaist attitudes (391), it is neither gratuitous nor perhaps far off the mark. For *391* was the name of Francis Picabia's review, which in turn was an adaptation of the *291* of Alfred Steiglitz, the American avant-garde photographer.[70] It is not far off the mark, although perhaps slightly exaggerated, because the lack of cohesion between the individuals connected with dada became more and more apparent until the final dissolution of dada in July of 1923.

All of the preceding remarks about *Le Manifeste sur l'amour faible et l'amour amer*—the insistence on the spontaneous and the fortuitous, the pose of idiocy, the nihilistic attitude, and the hint of possible internal dissentions—make this along with the 1918 manifesto a key dada pronouncement, providing invaluable information on the aims and techniques of dada. They are especially helpful because they define dada during the dada period and are undistorted by the personal animosities which have subsequently arisen among former dadaists, clouding their statements about the movement.

Little need be said about the *annexe* "How I became charming, sympathetic and delicious" and the concluding syllogism colonial and its nine lines of nonsense:

Personne ne peut échapper au sort
Personne ne peut échapper à DADA

Il n'y a que DADA qui puisse vous faire échapper
au sort.

Vous me devez: FR 943,50

Plus d'ivrognes!
Plus d'aéroplanes!
Plus de vigueur!
Plus de voies urinaires!
Plus d'énigmes! [71]

[No one can escape destiny
No one can escape DADA
Dada alone can enable you to escape destiny

You owe me 943.50 francs

No more drunks!
No more airplanes!
No more vigor!
No more urinary passages!
No more enigmas!]

Through the *sept manifestes DADA,* Tzara has re-
vealed an extremely provocative attitude toward all established values and especially toward logic. The battle
lines are drawn by these manifestoes, which represent a
determined attempt to discredit logic and to discredit
language as it is traditionally used. In lieu of these shop-
worn articles, Tzara offers spontaneity, gratuitousness,
and aggressiveness, inviting us to enter his circus tent of
delirium. Dada is presented as a *prise de position,* an attitude of negation with respect to art and society. It remains a noisily incoherent but significant protest against
formalism in the arts, and it is fundamentally a remon-
strance against rationality itself.

LAMPISTE n. Personne qui, dans une gare, un théâtre, une usine, est chargée de l'entretien des lampes. ‖ *Fig.* Personne qui, dans une entreprise, dans une administration, ou, *par extens.*, dans la société, n'assume que des responsabilités très réduites, dispose de peu de pouvoir, et sur qui les supérieurs, les puissants, font retomber le poids de leurs fautes.

LAMPISTERIE n. f. Industrie, commerce du lampiste ; ce qui concerne l'entretien des appareils d'éclairage. ‖ Endroit où l'on garde, répare, entretient les lampes d'un établissement, d'une gare. d'une mine.

Figure 5. Larousse definitions of "Lampiste" and "Lampisterie."

2 The Critical Illumination of the *Lampisteries*

« Le reste, nommé *littérature*, est dossier de l'imbécillité humaine pour l'orientation des professeurs à venir. »[1]

The dada years for Tzara were not entirely devoted to noisy confrontations with hostile audiences. His strident oral messages are complemented by almost two dozen articles on art and poetry which have been collected and published as *lampisteries* in the volume containing the *sept manifestes*. These articles first appeared in various literary magazines from July, 1917, through January, 1924. The title chosen by Tzara is curious, inasmuch as a *lampisterie* is defined by the Larousse dictionary as a place where lighting fixtures are kept and repaired. Thus the lampisteries could be old odds and ends, leftovers, or perhaps Tzara could also be suggesting that the articles on Guillaume Apollinaire, Pierre Reverdy, Pierre Albert-

Birot, Francis Picabia, le comte de Lautréamont, etc., are an attempt to preserve their creative light. A *lampiste* is also a kind of railroad night watchman. This has given rise to the use of *lampiste* in French to signify any poor, insignificant individual. Tzara thus may be describing himself very modestly as an unimportant worker in the SNCF of aesthetics. The enterprise itself, however, is not unimportant. An unpublished introduction by Tzara to the *lampisteries* states that a common thread, uniting him with artists treated in these collected articles was the desire to "build up a new world on the debris of the old." He is once again joined in this enterprise by co-workers André Breton and Louis Aragon. Their most important critical articles on other poets, painters, and on aesthetics in general, did, however, appear after the demise of dada, Breton's *Le Surréalisme et la Peinture* [2] (which also treats dada) being published in 1928, and Aragon's *La Peinture au Défi* [3] coming two years later in 1930. Aragon's *Project for a History of Contemporary Literature*,[4] which appeared in *Littérature*, new series, no. 4, September 1922, would have been, if completed at this time, an invaluable and interesting source for the study of aesthetics during the second decade of this century. Its table of contents covers the period from the 1911 robberies in the Louvre (including the theft of the Mona Lisa and other works, for which Apollinaire was suspected and forced to spend nine days in prison) to the conclusion which treats "The State of Mind in 1922" and "How Dada didn't save the world."

Thus Tzara's dada criticism has some importance because it is fairly unusual. Does his perception as a critic match his energy as a propagandist for the dada movement and dada state of mind? Marcel Janco, painter and member of the Zurich dadaist group, answers this question affirmatively. "His gift for recognizing the relationships between society, historical period, and art qualify him for playing a decisive role in contemporary art criticism." [5] René Lacôte also attests Tzara's importance as a critic.

> Tzara has carefully analyzed, explained, and with a critical point of view, justified his attitude at each turning point and at each determining moment of his life and related it to all the revelations which have come about through the art and thought of his time. In so doing, for years he has put explosive ideas into circulation whose very diverse ramifications (after the willfully provoked scandal . . .) are found in the liveliest of contemporary literature.[6]

The "explosive" ideas are contained in the *manifestes DADA,* the major articles in dada and surrealist reviews, in *Le Surréalisme et l'Après-Guerre,* and in his prefaces to works of other artists. The artists who have most attracted his critical attention are Francis Picabia, Pablo Picasso, Henri Rousseau, Tristan Corbière, Arthur Rimbaud, François Villon, François Rabelais, Paul Eluard, and Guillaume Apollinaire.

In order to study the dada criticism of Tzara, let us examine rather closely two representative *lampisteries,* the "note sur l'art nègre," and "francis picabia," and conclude with general remarks about the other critical articles written by Tzara between 1917 and 1924.

At the Cabaret Voltaire there were frequent "African Nights" which would include the dadaists' version of African poetry and music. Long after the dada period Tzara explained the underlying reasons for this early interest in primitive art.

Aux préoccupations esthétiques d'Apollinaire qui considérait l'art comme un *produit* plus ou moins intentionnel de l'homme détachable en quelque sorte de sa nature intime, DADA opposait une conception plus large où l'art des peuples primitifs, imbriqué dans les fonctions sociales et religeuses, apparaissait comme l'expression même de leur vie. DADA, qui préconisait la « spontanéité dadaïste », entendait faire de la poésie une manière de vivre bien plus que la manifestation accessoire de l'intelligence et de la volonté. Pour lui, l'art était une des formes, communes à tous les hommes, de cette activité poétique dont la racine profonde se confond avec la structure primitive de la vie affective. DADA a essayé de mettre en pratique cette théorie reliant l'art nègre africain et océanien, à la vie mentale et à son expression immédiate . . . en organisant des SOIREES NEGRES de danse et de musique improvisées. Il s'agissait pour lui de retrouver, dans les profondeurs de la conscience, les sources exaltantes de la fonction poétique.[7]

[To the aesthetic preoccupations of Apollinaire, who considered art to be a more or less intentional *product* of man, disconnected in a way from his inner nature, DADA opposed a broader concept, in which the art of primitive peoples was an integral part of their social and religious functions and appeared as the very expression of their life. DADA, which advocated "dadaist spontaneity" meant to make of poetry a way of life much more than the incidental expression of intelligence and will. For DADA, art was one of the forms, common to all men, of that poetic activity whose profound roots mingle with the primitive structure of affective life. DADA tried to put that theory into practice, joining African Negro and Oceanic art with mental life and with its immediate expression . . . by organizing NEGRO SOIREES of improvised dance and music. It was for dada a matter of recapturing in the depths of consciousness the exalting sources of the function of poetry.]

This key statement points out the significance of dada's preoccupation with primitive art. The *first* expression of this important aspect of dada was Tzara's "Note 6 sur l'art nègre," which appeared in *Sic* in the September–October issue of 1917, and which was included with slight changes in the *lampisteries* as "Note sur l'art nègre." This was Tzara's initial contribution to *Sic,* the important art nouveau publication to which Apollinaire contributed several poems and articles. *Sic* was a review which expressed a mixture of cubist and futurist ideas—ideas which later would be violently repudiated by Tzara. The "Note on Negro Art" is important for two reasons. First, it shows the interest in primitive art which Tzara continued

thereafter to evince,[8] and it also shows that he was somewhat intrigued at this time with the cubist aesthetic,
being perhaps under the spell of Apollinaire with whom
he was corresponding. As we have seen, he vigorously
rejects cubism in his 1918 manifesto. The title "Note 6
sur l'art nègre" was a typical dada mystification, there
being no previous five notes.

Tzara begins this note by saying: "L'art nouveau est
en première ligne concentration, angle de la pyramide
. . ."[9] [The new art is first of all line concentration,
angle of the pyramid . . .] This describes the opposition
of the new and angular lines to the softness and *courbe*
of the lines in many previous works. Tzara rejects the
warmth, luxuriance, and sensuality found in many works
in favor of ". . . clarity which is direct."[10] Describing
the approaches to this clarity, he states: ". . . nous avons
d'abord déformé, puis décomposé l'objet, nous nous
sommes approchés de sa surface, nous l'avons pénétrée."[11]
[We have first of all distorted and decomposed the
object, we have approached its surface, we have pene-
trated it.] This is as close as Tzara would ever come to
cubism. It might be stated that the main distinction between the method here described and that of the cubists
is in the "penetration" of the object. Rather than a new,
simultaneous description of the whole surface, Tzara calls
for an *enfoncement*, a "plunging into."

In another key sentence he asserts: "Les influences de
nature étrangère qui s'entremêlaient sont les lambeaux

d'une doublure de la Renaissance encore accrochés à l'âme de nos prochains. . . ." [12] [The influences of a foreign nature which intermingled are the shreds of a Renaissance lining still fastened to the soul of our fellow men.] He is calling for the delineation of an object, *tout nu,* stripped of any references which it may have gathered. This will often necessitate new objects; the sunset, too heavily charged with associations, will have to give way to the spark plug. Tzara and dada are obviously at opposite poles from Renaissance and from impressionist art. To underscore the differences between the traditional concept of art and the new concept, influenced by primitive art, Tzara uses the image of two brothers, one a tattered and ineffectual product of traditionalism, and the other a wonderfully naïve and imaginative child who is as creative as his brother is sterile. The latter, still clinging to the old forms, is described as having a soul "aux branches aiguës, noires d'automne." [13] [with sharp-pointed black branches of autumn.] The chilly sterility of this outlook could not be more pronounced. The other brother is ". . . laughing, naïve and good." [14] This naïveté reflects a cult of childishness which was particularly strong among the dadaists and their precursors. The essential dada traits are those found also in children: those of wonder, refusal (one thinks of Rimbaud's "deafer than children's minds"), [15] spontaneity, unpredictability, and the will to destroy. This good brother laughs. Tzara, who is here the advocate of humor, was to retain this quality in his own works, the *blague* being nearly always present in his pre-Marxist writings. The world which permitted global war had, in the opinion of the dadaists, relinquished its right to be taken seriously. Consequently the world's absurdity would be opposed by dada's own foolishness. Tzara mentions that the good brother, who is naïve and humor-loving, and who lives in Africa and "the bracelets of the oceanic islands," ". . . concentre sa vision sur la tête, la taille dans du bois dur comme le fer, patiemment, sans se soucier du rapport conventionnel entre la tête et le reste du corps." [16] [. . . concentrates his vision on the head, hews it patiently out of a wood hard as iron without bothering himself about the conventional relationship between the head and the rest of the body.] Symmetry and measure were not, in Tzara's opinion, primary factors in African or Oceanic art, nor were they considered important by the dadaists. More fruitful was the quality of gratuitousness, since "en travaillant, les relations nouvelles se rangent par degrés de nécessité; ainsi naquit l'expression de la pureté." [17] [by working, new relationships draw themselves up by degrees of necessity; in this way the expression of purity was born.] The weary and conventional relationships, shreds of a Renaissance lining, are discarded. New relationships come of themselves through a free juxtaposition of apparently dissimilar objects, for as Tzara says: "Dans l'homme je vois la lune, les plantes, le noir, le métal, l'étoile, le poisson. Que les éléments cosmiques glissent symétriquement. Déformer, bouillir." [18] [In man I see the moon, the plants, blackness, metal, the star, the fish. Let the cosmic elements slip symetrically. Distort, boil.] This may be a fine poetic description of some primitive art. It is most certainly one of the best descriptions of Tristan Tzara's own poetic universe in which the whirling of the cosmos and the confusion of animal, mineral, and vegetable are ever present. It is significant that this vision is not born in the mind, but in the mouth. "La bouche contient la puissance de l'obscurité, substance invisible, bonté, peur, sagesse, création, feu." [19] [The mouth contains the power of the obscure, invisible substance, goodness, fear, wisdom, creation, fire.] The mouth has only to speak to give birth to all these concepts, the mind not being involved. As Tzara said in his *manifeste sur l'amour faible et l'amour amer,* "Thought is made in the mouth." Primitive art, like dada, was in his eyes founded on spontaneous and irrational creation.

The "note sur l'art nègre" concludes with the affirmation: "Personne n'a vu si clairement que moi ce soir. . . ." [20] [No one has seen so clearly as I this evening.] Many readers of *Sic,* disoriented by this poetic apology for primitive art, must have been left with an entirely different opinion. Tzara appears to have had an aversion to saying anything clearly at this period in his career. However, an unhurried reading of the text, combined with a familiarity with his artistic theories, reveals several basic ideas that help to explain dada's attitude toward primitive art: its wish to de-form the object depicted in order to penetrate its inner meaning, its choice to portray things not heavily charged with common associations, and its desire to create with childlike spontaneity. It is interesting to note that dada, which Tzara in his *sept manifestes* had resolutely maintained was anti-historical, reaches out to African Negro and Oceanic art as its spiritual ancestors. If dada loses in this process its claim to originality, which is at best tenuous considering its borrowings from both cubists and futurists, it nevertheless gains stature in being presented as a movement with roots in a very productive past.

The second representative *lampisterie* which I should like to study is "francis picabia." This first appeared in *Littérature* in December, 1919, and was used as the preface for Picabia's *Unique Eunuque* which the Galerie au Sans-Pareil in Paris published in April, 1920. Tzara also wrote a short note on Picabia which appeared in *Dada 4 et 5* in May, 1919. In addition to these short but interesting articles on Picabia, the best source books for material on this flamboyant personality are Michel Sanouillet's *Picabia*,[21] his integral re-edition of *391*,[22] and the work *Aires Abstraites*,[23] by Picabia's widow.

Picabia was probably brought to the attention of the Zurich dadaists through his review, *391*, and his *Poèmes et Dessins de la Fille née sans Mère*, which appeared in Lausanne in 1918. Mme Picabia relates that her husband received a letter from Tzara in the name of a "comité directeur" shortly after the publication of the *Poèmes et*

Figure 6. Some of the collaborators of *391*, Paris, 1921. *Bottom row:* Tristan Tzara, Céline Arnauld, Francis Picabia, André Breton. *Middle row:* Benjamin Péret, Paul Dermée, Philippe Soupault, Georges Ribemont-Dessaignes. *Top row:* Louis Aragon, Théodore Fraenkel, Paul Eluard, Clément Pansaers(?), Emmanuel Faÿ. Reproduced from Michel Sanouillet, *Francis Picabia et 391*, vol. 1, p. 141 (Paris: Eric Losfeld, 1966).

Figure 7. Reveil Matin, Francis Picabia, 1919 (drawing). Title page for *Dada 4–5,* May 15, 1919. Reproduced from Robert Motherwell, *The Dada Painters and Poets,* p. 130 (New York: Wittenborn, Schultz, Inc., 1951), with the permission of Mrs. Barnett Malbin.

Figure 8. La Pomme de Pins, 1922 (publicity flyer). Reproduced from Michel Sanouillet, *Francis Picabia et 391,* vol. 2, p. 221 (Paris: Eric Losfeld, 1966).

Dessins, inviting him to join the dada group. "Very amused by the name 'Dada' which we had never heard and by the enthusiastic tone of the letter, he replied to the invitation and we went to Zurich in early 1919." [24] Jean Arp mentions that he and Tzara, forming a welcoming committee, went to the Hotel Elite where they found the newly arrived Picabia busily dissecting an alarm clock. The alarm clock is one of the keys to Picabia's work. His sketch of the complicated innards of a clock forms the title page of *Dada 4 et 5*, and indeed one might contend that the comparison of the clocks of Picabia and those of Dali provides a revealing insight into differences between dada and surrealism. Picabia's clocks, stripped of their former importance, all crazily jangling springs, are absurd but they are essentially real things. Dali's surrealist time pieces are transformed by the artist's subconscious and infused with magical new significance. They continue to keep a new kind of sur-real time.

After a brief stay in Zurich, the Picabias went to Paris where they were eventually joined by Tzara. Picabia participated actively in the Parisian dadaist activities but, becoming progressively disenchanted, he renounced dada with his customary *brio* in 1921. This break is signaled by the attack on Tzara and other dadaists which appeared in Picabia's *La Pomme de Pins*.[25] Tzara answered Picabia in kind in his *Cœur à Barbe*.[26] This, in brief, gives some idea of the blustery relationship between these men. The *lampisterie* which we will study was written in 1919, at a time when both were still good friends.

The text will be studied closely, with emphasis not only on the ideas but also on the free poetic approach taken by Tzara. The first sentences immediately reveal this approach.

Les myriapodes philosophiques ont cassé des jambes de bois ou de métal, et même des ailes, entre les stations Vérité-Réalité. Il y avait toujours quelque chose d'insaisissable: LA VIE.[27]

[The philosophic myriapoda have broken wooden or metal legs, and even wings, between the Truth and Reality stations. There was always something which got away: LIFE.]

Tzara, the antiphilosopher, derides philosophy for not having found definitive answers. One of the parallels between dadaists and existentialists is found in a shared contempt for systems which are preoccupied with everything but the conduct of human life itself. As Richard Huelsenbeck remarks in his provocative article, "Dada and Existentialism,"

When Sartre says that man wants to be God, it means no more than that he has realized that the creative force within him is identical with the universal creative force. In other words, man is no longer the product of some conventional morality. He can no longer suffer himself to be pushed this way and that by political, economic, or religious catchphrases. He is what he is because he has become aware of his own value.[28]

Tzara included Picabia with himself as antiphilosopher and hater of "catch-phrases." Art itself had become a "catch-phrase" and as such was to be destroyed by "les aventures sans remords qui s'introduisent en art par ses moyens pour le détruire lentement, réveillent la cendre dans le noyau, intérêts réciproques, insinuations et obstacles système mouvement DADA."[29] [the unremorseful adventures which infiltrate art through its own means to destroy it slowly, reawaken the cinder in the core, reciprocal interests, insinuations and obstacles system movement DADA.] This is a reasonably explicit answer to the question of antiphilosophers and anti-aestheticians: "But why do you write" Tzara states that he and Picabia attack "fine" art *through* art, and that this Trojan horse technique is the dada technique *par excellence*. He is categorical in saying that his literary adventure is justified because it is aimed at destroying conventional art. Other writers, asked to justify their activity by the review *Littérature*, expressed a feeling of shame for their profession. Most, at this time, were openly apologetic about writing. It is worth noting that many of the same writers had evolved far enough politically by 1933 to answer the new question: "For *whom* [my italics] do you write?"[30] Only a few, such as Pierre Albert-Birot, former editor of *Sic* and author of a dada play, *Le Bondieu*, could answer flippantly: "Why, for those who can read of course."[31] Philippe Soupault, who has never ceased believing in dada, showed the old spirit by replying: "You know the inscription you read on many walls: 'S. . . on whomever reads this.' " [32] This reply could not have pleased Louis Aragon, convinced communist at this time and editorial secretary, who probably wanted to hear that one wrote for the masses.

Picabia and Tzara are also saying, "S. . . on whomever reads this."

> Mais donner à une blague le caractère d'éternité et lui préparer l'exclusivité de la faim, est ridicule, bonjour naïf d'onaniste, musique salutiste, prétention mélangée, succursale de bourgeois chatouillant l'art.[33]

> [But to give eternal status to a joke and to prepare for it the exclusivity of hunger is ridiculous, naive onanist greeting, Salvation Army hymns, mixed pretention, branch office of bourgeois tickling art.]

Art is a joke which is sterile, pompous, and tainted by bourgeois values. It should be remembered that Tzara would not hesitate to apply this statement to dada itself, if it ran the risk of becoming another "school" without vigor, a large but meaningless noise, or a branch office of bourgeois culture like cubism or futurism. Nothing deserves the "status of eternity."

> Le besoin de chercher des explications à ce qui n'a pas d'autre raison que d'être *fait*, simplement, sans discussions, avec le minimum de critère ou de critique, ressemble à la self-cleptomanie: loger perpétuellement ses propres objets dans des poches différ-

entes. On s'arrange d'habitude aussi pour constituer une collection d'une spécialité morale quelconque, pour la commodité
des jugements. Les hommes sont pauvres parce qu'ils se volent
eux-mêmes. Ce n'est pas la difficulté de comprendre la vie
moderne qui est en cause, mais ils volent des éléments à leur
propre personnalité.[34]

[The need to find explanations for that which has no other
reason than to *be made*, simply, without discussion, with the
minimum of criteria or criticism, is like self-cleptomania: per-
petually putting your own things in different pockets. It's in
this way that you usually arrange to make up some sort of
moral specialty, for the commodity of judgments. Men are
poor because they rob themselves. It's not the difficulty of understanding modern life which is involved; but they steal the
elements of their own personality.]

The first idea expressed here is the attitude to be taken
before a work, and, I assume, this applies particularly to
Picabia's work of the dada period. Tzara is unequivocal
in declaring that there are works which one should not
try to reason out. In the catalogue for Picabia's 1920 exhibition, he reiterated this, saying:

. . . ne cherchez rien dans ces tableaux, le sujet et le moyen
sont: Francis Picabia. Le tableau dada est une douche uni-
verselle à l'eau rouge. La nature est ce qui sort des yeux et
des doigts—librement—elle a un numéro de téléphone un
appartement au Champ de Mars, une voiture de 85 HP,

comme l'amitié et la conversation filtrée par le filet du tissu cérébral.[35]

[. . . don't look for anything in these paintings. The subject and the means are Francis Picabia. A dada painting is a universal shower in red water. Nature is what comes freely from the eyes and fingers. It has a telephone number an apartment on the Champ de Mars, a high-powered car, like friendship and conversation filtered by the net of cerebral tissue.]

Tzara is pleading here for gratuity in the artistic work. Instead of the normal, rational, and critical attitude, he advocates a completely open and subjective acceptance of the work which is not *about* anything. He asserts that the need for classification impoverishes. This enlargement of the personality, the refusal to be confined by reason, reveals an attitude which will logically carry Tzara into the surrealist camp a few years after writing the article on Picabia whose poetic world is described in the following manner:

PICABIA. La parole fertilise le métal. Bolide ou roue, urubu, ouragan ourlé et ouvert, il laisse dormir ses sentiments dans un garage. Je place un hibou dans un hexagone, chante en hexamètres, use les angles, crie *à bas* et abuse. La géométrie est sèche, vieille. J'ai vu jaillir une ligne autrement. Une ligne jaillie tue les théories; il ne nous reste que le besoin de chercher l'aventure dans la vie des lignes. Œuvre personnelle, celle qui fuit l'absolu. Et vit. S'évade. De la sève muette.[36]

[PICABIA. The word fructifies the metal. Racing car or wheel, urubu, hurricane, hemmed and unhampered. He lets his feelings sleep in a garage. I put an owl in an hexagon, sing in hexameters, use angles, shout *down with* and abuse. Geometry is dry, old. I've seen a line spring up in a different manner. A wayward line kills theories. All that remains for us is the need to search for adventure in the life of lines. A personal work, the one which flees the absolute. And lives, and escapes. Mute sap.]

This free and poetic description of Picabia's works is particularly rich in meaning. In the *Unique Eunuque,* words and metal are interchangeable; words are metal, hard and not comforting. Tzara, in the *sept manifestes DADA,* had also urged the artist to be severe and uncompromising. He was calling for an artist like Picabia who would concentrate on depicting the inner workings of machines.

Mirroring the absurdity of Picabia's creation is the seeming linguistic absurdity of Tzara. The series of words, "ou roue urubu ouragan ourlé et ouvert" is a game of alliteration. "Urubu" does bring Jarry to mind, however, and there are striking resemblances between Picabia and the author of *Ubu Roi.* The physical similarities are apparent, both men being short and powerful, and their works express a common aggressive quality.

When Tzara says of Picabia "He lets his feelings sleep in a garage," he seems to be suggesting that Picabia, being a modernist, rejects sentimentality. The mention of the garage, like the reference to Ubu, could be gratuitous but

MERCER 85 HP

Les 2 exhibitionnistes intoxiqués
par l'abus de l'automobile

(Le Populaire. — 17 mai 1920*)*

Messieurs les révolutionnaires vous avez les idées aussi étroites que celles d'un petit bourgeois de Besançon.   Francis PICABIA.

Figure 9. Picabia and Tzara, 1920. Originally appeared in Picabia's review *Cannibale*, no. 2, May 25, 1920. Reproduced from Michel Sanouillet, *Francis Picabia et 391*, vol. 2, p. 203 (Paris: Eric Losfeld, 1966).

it is nevertheless appropriate because the wealthy Picabia enjoyed expensive automobiles which he had modified for maximum speed. His white Mercedes was familiar to the avant-garde. A frequent passenger in Picabia's racing cars was Guillaume Apollinaire, who had dubbed Picabia an "orphic cubist" in his *Peintres Cubistes*.[37] Comparing some of Apollinaire's remarks about Picabia with Tzara's points up some of the essential differences between cubism and dada. Apollinaire insists on the importance of the geometrical vision. "The geometrical aspect which has so vividly struck those who have seen the first scientific canvases came from the fact that the essential reality was rendered with great purity and the visual and anecdotal accident was eliminated from them." [38] Tzara also rejects the "visual and anecdotal accident," but for him geometry is "dry, old. I've seen a line spring up in a different manner." Geometry is order, calm, and precision. Tzara, who wished to promote the idiot, rejects geometry categorically. This is all the more interesting in the light of the fact that he had originally come to Zurich as a mathematics student, and traces of this early scientific bent can be found in the numerous formulas of *La Première Aventure céleste*. A dada line is haphazard, unpredictable and anarchistic. This kind of line, as formed by Picabia, would discredit the old theories and shake confidence in the old beliefs. Something like this was not only taking place in art at this time but also in physics, as the established theories were being tested by totally new ideas.[39]

Picabia's work, like the other dada productions, is a "personal work which flees the absolute." Like its author it is without pretense, probably because it is not written with posterity in mind. It lives, as Tzara says, because it is evasive, escaping classification, criticism, and comprehension itself. Tzara describes it as being "mute sap," life-giving but devoid of a message. In this way Picabia's work would seem to be typical of that twentieth century art of which it has been said that it follows the path from the silent to the absolutely mute.[40]

Tzara expresses his delight at not finding charm or sentimentality in Picabia's drawings because, as he says, " 'charme' et 'joli' s'appliquent au clair de lune, aux sentiments, aux tableaux qui chantent et aux chansons qui voient, collent aux traditions, s'infusent parmi les pompiers et parmi les peintres." [41] ["charm" and "pretty" apply to moonlight, to sentiments, to paintings that sing and songs that see, and stick to traditions, infusing themselves among the pompous and the painters.] It is amusing to see how Tzara, who often uses the word charm with derision, is usually described as a very charming person.[42] Nevertheless, this is an attack on natural beauty and on the banality of emotions brought on by moonlight. Apollinaire had said in speaking of Picabia's canvases, "They can't lay claim to Poussin's affirmation that 'painting has no other goal than delectation and visual joy.' They are ardent and wild works." [43] Tzara says roughly the same thing about Picabia. For Tzara, art is not beauty of description, but it *is* discovery and adventure. It can even be anti-beauty as illustrated by Picabia's *American Girl,* which is simply the sketch of a light bulb. Tzara states that Picabia has freed himself from the necessity to celebrate natural beauty, and he chides the cubists and the futurists for their inability to do likewise.

Les peintres cubistes et futuristes, qui devraient laisser vibrer leur joie d'avoir libéré l'apparence d'un extérieur encombrant et futile, deviennent scientifiques et proposent l'académie. Propagation théorique de charognes, pompe pour le sang. Il y a des paroles qui sont aussi des légions d'honneur. A la chasse des gros mots qui assurent le bonheur de l'humanité, du prestige prestidigitateur de prédilections prodigieuses pour le plaisir de ceux qui payent. Chapitre: respect de la soupe.[44]

[The cubist and futurist painters, who should let their joy of liberation from the encumbering and futile exterior of appearance break out, are becoming scientific and propose their candidacy for the academy. Theoretic propagation of cadavers, blood pump. There are words which are also government decorations, hunting for portentuous words which assure the happiness of humanity, and of the prestige prestidigator of prodiguous predilections for the pleasure of those who pay. Chapter: respect for the soup.]

Tzara had flirted with the cubists in writing for *Sic* and he had obviously been influenced by the futurists who advocated *bruitism* and simultaneous poetry, but in this

Figure 10. American Girl, Francis Picabia, n.d. (painting). Reproduced from Michel Sanouillet, *Francis Picabia et 391*, vol. 1, p. 49 (Paris: Eric Losfeld, 1966).

study of Picabia, he does not hesitate to attack these movements, stating that while the cubists and futurists should
have been delighted to have broken some artistic tram-
mels, they in fact had lost their healthy iconoclasm and
had become nothing more than artistic schools. Even their
vocabulary had lost its vigor, the futurists and cubists
using words which were nothing better than government
decorations. Tzara and Picabia, as true dadaists, refused
to put their work in the service of the establishment, although a few years later, Picabia would, for financial
reasons, do a series of erotic canvases for wealthy North
Africans. At this stage in his career, however, Tzara re-
gards Picabia as free from the temptation of vile lyricism
and the anecdotal, for, as Tzara says:

> Les idées empoisonnent la peinture; si le poison porte un
> nom sonore de gros ventre philologique, l'art devient con-
> tagion, et, si l'on se réjouit de cette intestine musicalité, le
> mélange devient danger pour les hommes propres et sobres.[45]

> [Ideas poison painting. If the poison carries a sonorous name
> from the big philological belly, art becomes contagion; and
> if one rejoices in that intestinal musicality, the mixture be-
> comes a danger for decent and serious people.]

There are no ideas in Picabia's work, no anecdotal or
facile lyricism. "Picabia a réduit la peinture à une formulation sans problèmes. . . ."[46] [Picabia has reduced painting to a formulation without problems. . . .] The
painting is simply a thing and not the product of a strug-

gle with problems of light and dark or perspective. Standing by itself, it defies rational analysis.

> . . . chacun y trouvera les lignes de sa vie,
> qui vont avec le temps en chemin de fer et par
> téléphone sans fil
> s'il sait regarder sans se demander pourquoi une
> tasse ressemble à un sentiment.[47]

> [. . . each person will find in it the lines of his life
> which accompany time by train and by
> wireless telephone
> if he knows how to look without asking himself why
> a cup resembles a sentiment.]

The work of art is not totally useless. There is something to be seen in it, but the manner of looking must be uncritical. One must allow free rein to the irrational message, which differs for each spectator.

In studying Picabia, Tzara has pleaded the cause of "terrorism" in the arts.[48] Picabia is described as an orthodox dadaist, his literary work and his painting posing a threat to the traditional concept of art. He is congratulated by Tzara for not prostituting his talent to the bourgeoisie and for creating works which are untamed and beyond understanding. He is a geometer rather than a sentimentalist, but he is a wildly free geometer. His free spirit rejects both verbal and plastic clichés. In thus describing Picabia, Tzara has further elaborated some of the basic tenets of dadaism.

The other *lampisteries* reveal a rejection of the artistic movements of romanticism and impressionism and propose new directions for art. They both oppose and propose —this latter tendency has perhaps not been sufficiently insisted upon in studies of dadaism. One short text illustrates these two tendencies:

Humidité des âges passés. Ceux qui se nourrissent de larmes sont contents et lourds . . . Mais pour l'abondance et l'explosion, il [le poète] sait allumer l'espoir AUJOURD'HUI . . . son désir bout pour l'enthousiasme, féconde forme de l'intensité.[49]

[Humidity of past ages. Those who feed on tears are satisfied and heavy . . . But for the abundance and explosion, he knows how to fire hope TODAY . . . his desire boils for enthusiasm, fruitful form of intensity.]

Sentimentality is again rejected by Tzara, and this is nowhere more fiercely expressed than in his "Note sur le comte de lautréamont ou le Cri." [50]

L'esprit de cet homme négatif, prêt à chaque instant à se laisser tuer par le carrousel du vent et piétiner par la pluie des météores, dépasse l'hystérie douceâtre de Jésus et d'autres moulins à vent infatigables, installés dans les somptueux appartements de l'histoire.[51]

[The spirit of that negative man, always ready to let himself be killed by the merry-go-round of the wind and trampled

by the shower of meteors, goes beyond the sweet hysteria of
Jesus and other indefatigable windmills, settled in the sump-
tuous apartments of history.]

The positive side of the *lampisteries* is seen in a poetic
quality which Tzara calls "cosmic" and which transcends
sentiment, uniting men with each other and with every
part of their environment.

Nous voulons rendre aux hommes la faculté de comprendre
que l'unique fraternité existe dans le moment d'intensité où
le beau et la vie concentrés sur la hauteur d'un fil de fer mon-
tent vers l'éclat . . . Nombreux sont les artistes qui ne cher-
chent plus les solutions dans l'objet et dans ses relations avec
l'extérieur; ils sont cosmiques ou primaires, décidés, simples,
sages, sérieux.[52]

[We want to give men the ability to understand that brotherhood exists only in the moment of intensity where beauty
and life, concentrated on the heights of a metal wire, ascend
toward the brilliance. . . . Numerous are the artists who
no longer look for solutions in the object and in its relationships with the exterior; they are cosmic or elemental, resolute,
simple, wise, serious.]

Tzara further defines "cosmic" as:

. . . une qualité essentielle de l'œuvre d'art. Parce qu'elle implique l'ordre qui est condition nécessaire à la vie de tout organisme. Les éléments multiples, divers et éloignés sont, plus

ou moins intensément, concentrés dans l'œuvre; l'artiste les recueille, les choisit, les range, en fait une construction ou une composition.[53]

[. . . an essential quality of the work of art. Because it implies order which is a necessary condition for the life of any organism. Multiple, diverse and distant elements are, more or less intensely, concentrated in the work; the artist collects them, selects, arranges, and makes from them a construction or composition.]

In a particularly important article on Pierre Reverdy,[54] Tzara further expounds on the "cosmic" in art and explains the reasons for rejecting the concept of art as it has existed since the Renaissance.

Depuis la Renaissance l'art fut: l'anecdote comme centre, comme principe, c'est-à-dire histoire racontée au richard pour éveiller en lui un "sentiment;" 64% de pitié, le reste: humilité, etc.[55]

[Since the Renaissance art has been the anecdote as the center, as principle; that is, a story told to a money-bags to awaken in him a "feeling;" 64% pity, the rest: humility, etc.]

Tzara objects to the kind of art produced under this system and to the kind of people who commissioned it. He calls "the detestable age which followed the quatrocento" an age in which art became a fancy brothel, catering to the rich and self-satisfied. Happily, a writer like

Pierre Reverdy does not continue this tradition in his work. One does not find there, according to Tzara, any pandering to man's wish to find himself the center of the universe, the measure of all things. There is, in fact, no hierarchy of being in Reverdy's works, where man is simply on a level with the rest of creation. Reverdy is a perfect illustration of the practitioner of "cosmic art" whose principles Tzara describes in the following manner:

"Il y a deux principes dans le cosmique:

1. Donner une importance égale à chaque objet, être, matériau, organisme de l'univers.
2. Accentuer l'importance de l'homme, grouper autour de lui, pour les lui subordonner, les êtres, les objets, etc. . . .

Le noyau de ce dernier principe est une méthode psychologique; le danger: le besoin de CORRIGER les hommes. Il s'agit de les laisser à ce qu'ils veulent devenir, des êtres supérieurs. Le poète se laisse entraîner au hasard de la succession et de l'impression. Pour le premier principe, ce besoin prend une nouvelle forme: ranger les hommes à côté des autres éléments, tels qu'ils sont, rendre les hommes MEILLEURS. Travailler en commun, anonymement, à la grande cathédrale de la vie que nous préparons; niveler les instincts de l'homme qui, si l'on accentuait trop la personnalité, prendraient des proportions babyloniennes de méchanceté et de cynisme." [56]

[There are two principles in the cosmic:

1. To give an equal importance to each object, being, material, organism of the universe.

2. To accentuate the importance of man, grouping around
   him in order to subordinate them to him, beings, objects,
   etc. . . .

The core of this latter principle is a psychological method;
the danger is the need to CORRECT men. It is a matter of
letting them become what they will, superior beings. The
poet lets himself be carried along by the chance of succession and impression. For the first principle, the need takes
another form: to place men alongside the other elements
just as they are, in order to make men BETTER. Work
together anonymously on the great cathedral of life which is
our project, even out man's instincts which, if the personality
were to be unduly stressed, would take on the proportions of
Babylonian evil and cynicism.]

This key statement illustrates a positive side of the dada
aesthetic, showing that beneath the pose of idiocy—at
least in Tzara's case—there was an underlying conviction
that a new kind of art could help men freely develop
their potential. The germ of a subsequent—and surrealist—theory of artistic creation is contained in this
particular *lampisterie*. Tzara, the dada *lampiste*, was not
so much stumbling in the dark as he was illuminating
what he considered to be the most significant contributions of his fellow artists from Picabia, Reverdy, Lautréamont and Apollinaire to primitive artists from Africa
to Oceania, who were all united as "travailleurs de l'obscurité et du verbe essentiels." [57] [workmen of the essential
obscurity and word.]

« Déboutonnez votre cerveau
aussi souvent que votre braguette. »
Odéon Theatre graffito, May 1968

PART TWO

The Surrealist
Adventure

Figure 11. The Surrealists, Valentine Hugo, 1934 (collage). Breton (three times), Char, Crevel, Unik, Tzara, Péret, Bunuel, and Ernst are included. Dedicated to Jacqueline Lamba, Breton's second wife. Reproduced from *Europe*, November-December 1968, p. 160.

3 "L'Essai sur la Situation de la Poésie"

Like Jean Tinguely's fantastic machine, dada seemed bent on destroying itself. The inner dissentions among its "391" directors gave proof that its anarchy could not be self-perpetuating, and the time came when dada was no longer anything but a four-franc cocktail that the Café Certa, a Parisian avant-garde hangout, offered along with a "Pick me Hup" or a "Kiss me Quick" at three francs and fifty centimes.

The death rattle of dada was heard on a July night in 1923 at the Théâtre Michel in Paris, although it must be admitted that since the Congrès de Paris, dada had been more or less moribund. On this occasion, Tzara's third play, *Le Cœur à Gaz*,[1] was to be presented. When Tzara's former friends, Louis Aragon, Benjamin Péret, and André Breton, came to sabotage the play, a furious fight broke out. Leaping up on the stage, Breton began to attack the actors, who were unable to fight back because they were rigidly encased in cardboard boxes designed by Sonia Delaunay. This scuffle marked the end of the original dada movement.

The personal differences between Tzara and Breton that hastened the demise of dada merit discussion because they furnish an insight into essential variances between dada and surrealism. As mentioned previously, André Breton attempted in 1922 to organize a "Congress of Paris" which was to give coherence to modernism in the arts. This congress was to hold sessions *under police protection* and observe parliamentary procedure, with the intention of giving direction to the various manifestations of modern art. It should be obvious how absurd this is from a dada point of view. Tzara naturally declined Breton's invitation to participate in the ill-fated congress. His polite refusal infuriated Breton, prompting him to attack Tzara openly, calling him a fraud and an *arriviste* and asserting that ". . . M. Tristan Tzara had no hand in the invention of Dada." [2] After attacking Tzara, Breton haughtily defended his own penchant for excommunications. "It's been said that I change people the way you change boots. Please be charitable and grant me this luxury. I can't always wear the same pair. When they don't fit me anymore I give them to my domestics." [3] Thus the stage was set for the public coronary suffered by the *Gas Operated Heart* and by dada as a movement. All that remained after the tumult were the shredded costumes, the broken seats, and the one prop: Marcel Duchamp's *Bicycle Wheel,* resting on a kitchen stool and symbolizing dada's intention to reduce art to the commonplace.

The transition from dada to surrealism has been likened to a government crisis in which the cabinet posts are rotated with the personnel remaining essentially the same. Tzara was one of the few exceptions to this, his quarrel with Breton keeping him on the periphery of surrealism until 1929. He could not share Breton's typically French desire for order, nor could Breton tolerate the continued buffooneries of dada. Surrealism is in part a semi-scientific attempt to explore and *chart* the unknown realms of the subconscious. *Le Premier Manifeste du Surréalisme* [4] is a striking example of this, in that it is a clear and reasonable statement of Breton's objectives and is far removed from the frivolities and strident obscenities of the *sept manifestes DADA.*

However, despite the difference between the two movements in orientation, it should be pointed out that several dada techniques as elaborated by Tzara were appropriated by the surrealists. Automatic writing is akin to "thought which is made in the mouth." In both cases the source is the subconscious, and they both may be termed *endophasie* or *langage intérieur.* In addition, the gratuitousness of dadaist poetry as expressed in Tzara's formula for a dada poem was retained by the surrealists, Breton asserting: "It is even possible to label 'Poem' what is obtained by the most gratuitous assemblage possible (let's observe syntax if you will) of captions and fragments of head-lines cut out of newspapers." [5]

Such basic similarities in attitude toward poetry would bring about a reconciliation between Tzara and Breton, once their tempers had cooled. This happened in 1929 when, in *Le Deuxième Manifeste Surréaliste*, Breton apologized to Tzara and praised his work. He likewise at times expressed real dadaist truculence toward society in such statements as: "The simplest surrealist act consists in going out in the street, revolvers in hand, and shooting at random as much as you wish into the crowd." [6] This certainly is reminiscent of dada, one of the Zurich dadaists, Richard Huelsenbeck, having already said that he wanted to make literature with a gun in his pocket. Another echo of dada is heard in Breton's attack on the family, the fatherland, and on religion. "Everything must be done, all means should be employed in order to ruin the ideas of *family, fatherland*, religion." [7] In addition to these attitudes, which had been of great importance to dada and whose expression must have drawn Tzara closer to the surrealists, there was the public apology offered by Breton to the founder of dada.

> . . . we feel the wish to render to a man from whom we have found ourselves separated for long years that justice that the expression of his thought still interests us, and to judge from what we still read from him, his preoccupations have not become foreign to us; given these conditions, there is perhaps

Figure 12. Loplop Introduces Members of the Surrealist Group, Max Ernst, 1930 (collage). Courtesy Museum of Modern Art, N.Y. Photo Suichi Sunami, N.Y.

reason to believe that our misunderstanding with him was not founded on anything so serious as we had thought.[8]

Breton even apologized in this manifesto for the riot that marked the end of dada. "I dare say that it is possible that Tzara was a victim of excessive biases on the occasion of the too famous representation of the *Cœur à Barbe*. . . ." [9] In inviting Tzara to join the surrealists, Breton praises his poetry.

> We believe in the efficacity of Tzara's poetry and we might go so far as to say that, along with surrealism, we consider it to be the only really *situated* poetry. When I speak of its efficacity, I mean to signify that it is operative in the vastest domaine and that it is a step taken today in the direction of human deliverance. When I say that it is situated, you understand that I contrast it with all poetic works which could just as well have been yesterday's or before that. . . . [10]

Breton's insistence on the word "situated" is significant because it introduces Tzara's first critical work under the aegis of surrealism, the "Essai sur la Situation de la Poésie," which appeared in *Le Surréalisme au Service de la Révolution 4* in December 1931. Tzara responded to Breton's generosity expressed in the Manifesto by joining with the surrealists and becoming one of the original members of the *SASDLR* group. Maturing with Breton (both were born in 1896), Tzara abandoned the adolescent revolt in favor of a constructive attempt to change the world.

Often Tzara is simply thought of as the leader of dada, and consequently his post-dada activity is overlooked. It should be understood that his thirties and forties were as productive as his twenties. His work from 1924 through the end of World War II establishes him as one of the major surrealist poets along with Breton and Eluard, and with Breton and Aragon as one of the most lucid interpreters of this movement. Let us now consider the important "Essai sur la Situation de la Poésie."

The basic significance of this first contribution by Tzara to *LSASDLR* is to be found in his unusual definition of poetry and in his application of this definition to a study of the literary origins of surrealism. Tzara's description of poetry, replete with references to Hegel, Jung, Lévy-Bruhl, and Marx, centers around the distinction between what he calls "poésie-activité de l'esprit" [poetry as mental activity] and "poésie-moyen d'expression" [poetry as means of expression]. For him there are two kinds of poetry, the first being a mental attitude which is not necessarily expressed in verse, and the second being verse writing. Tzara is scornful of the limitations of "poetry as means of expression." His wish is to integrate this into "poetry as mental state" in order to tap the common, although prearticulated, sentiments which belong to the whole human race. Thus, poetry, instead of being in the service of the wealthy and cultured, could become the expression of the aspirations of all men. At first it would seem that an attack on "poetry as means of expression" is the manifestation of an antisocial attitude, having as its goal the undermining of a very basic means of communication. This, however, is not the case. Tzara's motivation, eminently social and even humanistic, is the desire for human brotherhood—achieved on something other than the verbal level. Poetry could thus become, and indeed in Tzara's opinion *was* becoming, communication of the most immediate sort. It could assume a social function by bringing men together. René Lacôte has understood this effort on Tzara's part and he has described it clearly.

> There is certainly in this deep and permanent sentiment which links Tzara with what is the most essential or the most spontaneous in people, causing him to search everywhere for an expansion of the communicable realms, the most determining factor of his action.[11]

Tzara's definition of poetry, as we have seen, reveals a rejection of literature as expression of individual sentiments and an acceptance of literature as communal expression. It is an attack on traditional aesthetics and as such is obviously a continuation of dada, but it is in opposition to dada's nonsocial bias. In assessing this article by Tzara, we must first consider the significance of its extraliterary implications. We must then determine how Tzara justifies his definition of poetry by reference to psychology, philosophy, and anthropology. Finally, after we have looked at Tzara's application of his definition to a study of the evolution of modern French poetry, we must situate the essay itself with respect to other surrealist theory, in particular that set forth by André Breton.

The questioning of the validity of traditional aesthetics reached an acute stage with dada and surrealism. As early as 1924, the always perceptive Jacques Rivière said that he noticed a tendency which resulted in:

> . . . only writing as a last resort, or, at least, to assign extrinsic aims to writing, to literary creation. In spite of what certain short-sighted critics may think, no period, perhaps, has been as far away as ours from practicing "art for art's sake." It seems to me that we are witnessing a very serious crisis in the concept of what literature is.[12]

The "Essai sur la Situation de la Poésie" is a very clear illustration of that continuing crisis relating to the very concept of literature. It is, in fact, a sort of "Defense and Illustration" of the antipoetic, subverting what we normally think of as poetry. The dada manifestoes had shown this same contempt for poetry as a genre, a contempt also evident when, in rating poets for the review *Littérature*, Tzara gave the lowest possible grade to Baudelaire. This is particularly interesting when one thinks of the importance of both form and idea in Baudelaire's poetry. It is also worth noting that this open criticism of poetry as "means of expression" was published by Breton, a man who had an abiding respect for good verse. Ferdinand Alquié, an excellent interpreter of surrealism, notices this difference in opinion when he remarks that co-workers like Tzara helped to muddle the real value most surrealists have always given to poetry.[13]

There is no doubt that Tzara wished to change the old and restrictive concept of poetry as verse writing. For him, poetry is not simply a way of writing, but, infinitely more important, it is a mode of *thinking*. In a key statement, Tzara says: "Il est parfaitement admis aujourd'hui qu'on peut être poète sans jamais avoir écrit un vers, qu'il existe une qualité de poésie dans la rue, dans un spectacle commercial, n'importe où." [14] [It is clearly accepted today that you can be a poet without ever having written verse, and that there is a poetic quality in the street, in a commercial spectacle, anywhere.] This contention, contrary to what Tzara says, was not "clearly accepted" then, nor is it now. We often call a number of things "poetic" when they possess a certain quality of suggestiveness, an unusual affective charge, but this is certainly not poetry for anyone other than a confirmed literary terrorist like Tzara. Moreover, his assertion that poetry can be found in a "commercial spectacle" is only a restatement of some of the old "esprit nouveau" ideas and is particularly reminiscent of Apollinaire, who best expressed this idea in his poem "Zone."

> You read the handbills, catalogues, posters that sing
> out loud and clear—
> That's the morning's poetry, and for prose there
> are the newspapers,

> There are tabloids lurid with police reports,
> Portraits of the great and a thousand assorted stories.[15]

A word of caution should be given to those who would quickly assume that Tzara, like Apollinaire, is applying himself to the task of finding beauty in the commonplace. For him, it is not a question of beauty at all, and in this respect he attacks Proust, accusing him of trying to find poetry:

> . . . dans les pissotières, ce qui a entraîné l'éclosion d'une nouvelle génération de chercheurs de poésie-à-tout-prix-et-partout, l'appliquant à leurs propres productions dramatiques ou autres pour la retrouver au bout de cette chaîne excrémentielle où ignominieusement s'accouplent la justice et l'église.[16]

> [. . . in public urinals, which has given rise to a new generation of searchers for poetry-at-any-price-and-everywhere, applying it to their own or others' dramatic productions in order to find it again at the end of that excremental chain, where justice and the church ignominiously copulate.]

Although he believed that poetry could be found anywhere, Tzara opposed this search for the picturesque which often tends to induce a state of beatitude in the reader or viewer. The remarks about Proust refer to a passage in *A l'Ombre des Jeunes Filles en Fleurs* where the narrator relates his encounters with the "marquise" who

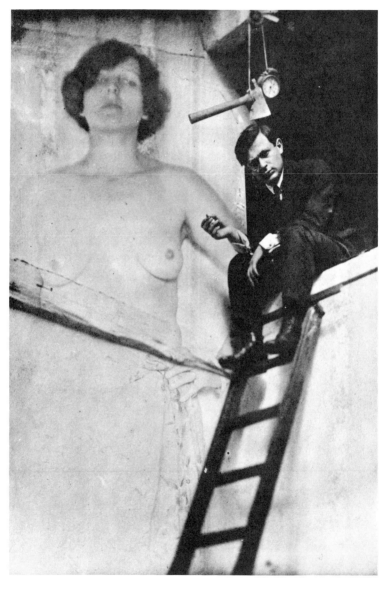

Figure 13. Tristan Tzara. Untitled, undated photo in the collection of Arturo Schwarz, Milan. Courtesy Arturo Schwarz.

was in charge of a public toilet. Proust's treatment of this
sort of theme perhaps shows the influence of Baudelaire
who said:

> He goes into the city, where, like the poet, his light
> Ennobles and gives purpose to the least thing in sight;
> Or, quietly, unattended, like a king, he calls
> At every palace, and visits all the hospitals.[17]

Tzara wants nothing to do with a concept of art as an
ennobling force. The classic idea of pure and enduring
beauty cannot be accepted by a critic who already is attracted by Marxism. He calls for a reassessment of the
concept of poetry. "Il s'agit d'analyser, ce que c'est que la
poésie à la lumière de nouvelles données . . . maintenant
que la prévision de bilan d'une activité dont nous ne con-
stituons qu'un chaînon devient possible." [18] [Now that
the beginnings of an evaluation of an activity of which
we only make up a link in the chain becomes possible, it's
a question of analyzing in the light of new data what
poetry is.] It is surprising to find Tzara admitting that
the group of which he has become a part belongs to any
general artistic evolution; however it will later be apparent that this evolution is in effect extra-literary.
Tzara's whole critical effort is toward a systematic de-
valuation of literature in favor of a state of mind which
would be absolutely free. In his judgment, literature has
validity only as mental liberation. To find confirmation

of this, Tzara uses Hegel's thought, wishing to demonstrate that certain natural principles, such as that of sudden and complete transformation from quantity to quality, may be applied to poetry as well. In the "Doctrine of Being," Hegel mentions sudden change in nature.

> Thus the temperature of water is in the first place, a point of no consequence in respect of its liquidity: still with the increase or diminution of the temperature of the liquid water, there comes a point where this state of cohesion suffers a qualitative change, and the water is converted into steam or ice.[19]

> Quantity, as we have seen, is not only capable of alteration, i.e., of increase or diminution: it is naturally and necessarily a tendency to exceed itself.[20]

Tzara claims that this kind of change is possible in the arts, that poetry *as a genre* is steadily giving way and will one day be replaced by what he calls "poetry as mental activity." The mention of Hegel in support of Tzara's thesis seems far-fetched, and is typical of a surrealist tendency to refer to science or philosophy for justification. The use of this particular Hegelian theory is original, but it is unconvincing, as the connection between poetic evolution and changes in nature are certainly not proved.

Tzara claimed that in 1931 most poetry was somewhere between verse writing and free mental activity, and that for it to make the radical change to the latter it would first have to free itself of language and structured form. In this assertion he goes much further than most other surrealists and stamps himself as one of the most radical of the linguistic anarchists. For him, language is the ultimate barrier to complete mental freedom and knowledge. For the Hegelian change from quantity to quality, from poetry as we know it to an entirely new concept, there must first be a triumph over words themselves.

Having used Hegel to support his theory of poetry, Tzara also mentions Jung as another witness. He first knew Jung when they were both in Zurich during World War I, and the distinction between "poésie-activité de l'esprit" and "poésie-moyen d'expression" is in part based on Jung's theories expressed in his *Metamorphosis and Symbols of Libido*, as in the chapter on "Two Kinds of Thinking."

> Thus we have two forms of thinking—*directed thinking* and *dream* or *phantasy thinking*. The first, working for communication with speech elements, is troublesome and exhausting; the latter, on the contrary, goes on without trouble, working spontaneously. . . . The first creates innovations, adaptations, imitates reality and seeks to act upon it. The latter, on the contrary, turns away from reality, sets free subjective wishes, and is, in regard to adaptation, wholly unproductive.[21]

Tzara had sensed this distinction from the beginnings of dada. His continued effort was in favor of "non-directed" thinking (although "other-directed" might be a better term) with the goal of undermining "directed" thought. He is in complete agreement with Jung, who further defines "the material with which we think as *language and speech concept,* a thing which has been used from time immemorial as something external, a bridge for thought, and which has a single purpose—that of communication." [22] Tzara, the archenemy of purely verbal communication, continually calls for the burning of the "bridge for thought" in favor of the thinking which is "un enchaînement, en apparence arbitraire, d'images; il est supra-verbal, passif et c'est dans sa sphère que se place le rêve, le penser fantaisiste et imaginatif et les rêveries diurnes." [23] [a seemingly arbitrary sequence of images; it is supra-verbal, passive, and it is in this sphere that dream, fantasy and imaginative thinking, and diurnal reveries take their place.] He claims that our Western civilization has impoverished us by destroying the flowering of "non-directed" thought. He further asserts that in a bourgeois, capitalistic society, one is normally forced to think to some purpose, but that it would be infinitely better to live, as do the primitives, a life of "daytime reveries," where life and thought would become poetry. Here Tzara was obviously influenced by Lucien Lévy-Bruhl's works on primitive mentality.

In a novel attempt to reconcile Jung and Marx and to put their thought in the service of his concept of poetry, Tzara links "directed" thought with capitalism, saying that the passage from primitive societies to capitalistic society has been accompanied by the impoverishing passage from dream to "directed" thought. He wishes to convince the reader that eventually, under a communistic form of society, "directed" thinking will wither away and man will recover the primitive wonder of a true dream state.

Whether or not this thesis has been substantiated by events in the communist world of the past quarter century, it is interesting to study Tzara's presentation of the poetic precursors of surrealism whom he believed would support his assertion that modern poetry was changing from a verse form to a free mental state. Comparing Tzara's precursors with those chosen by Breton will point up important differences in their respective attitudes toward poetry. In Tzara's opinion, the most significant writers have been those who have shown either through their works or their lives a fundamental antagonism to a bourgeois society and a capitalistic class. In this sense they are antisocial (or at least "anti" a *certain* society), but their ultimate efforts are directed toward serving humanity in general. Their works normally have in common the fact that they dissolve the normal, logical way of presenting man and his experience in the world. They tend to throw the reader off the logical track, to catch him off balance and to make him doubt both the validity of reason and the authenticity of a society which is enslaved by hyperorthodoxy and money.

This opposition to the reigning ideology may in general

take four forms. First, it may be a "pure" opposition, a social and political involvement. Second, it may tend to confuse by creating counterfeit and absurd worlds with laws of their own. Surrealism's precursors could also be those writers who have given up literature and taken refuge elsewhere—as in the dream, for instance. Finally, they could be writers who have attempted to destroy language itself. Obviously some of the poetic precursors of surrealism represent two or more of these possible attitudes.

Tzara groups the Marquis de Sade and the preromantics in the first group—i.e., those who directly oppose bourgeois society. He praises the preromantic temperament for having had:

> . . . la conscience qu'en dehors de l'exprimable et de l'exprimé, de la raison, un pays du merveilleux, encore inexploré, pouvait exister. L'amour des fantômes, des sorcelleries, de l'occultisme, de la magie, etc., du vice (en tant que facteur dissolvant de l'image conventionnelle du monde ou du point de vue de la liberté appliquée au domaine sexuel), du rêve, des folies, des passions, du folklore véritable ou inventé . . . des utopies sociales ou autres . . . de ce bric-à-brac des merveilles, aventures et mœurs des peuples sauvages, et généralement de tout ce qui sortait des cadres rigides, où l'on avait placé la beauté pour qu'elle s'identifiât avec l'esprit, ont naturellement préparé les romantiques à découvrir et imposer certains principes dont aujourd'hui encore les surréalistes peuvent fièrement se recommander.[24]

[. . . the awareness that aside from the expressable and the expressed and from reason, there could exist an as yet unexplored land of the marvelous. The love of phantoms, of witchcraft, of the occult, of magic, etc., of vice (as a factor which dissolves the conventional image of the world or from the point of view of liberty applied to the domain of the sexual), of dream, of extravagances, of passions, of true and invented folklore, . . . of social or other utopias . . . of that bric-à-brac of wonders, adventures, and ways of primitive peoples, and generally of everything that escaped the rigid limits where beauty had been placed so that it would become identified with the mind, have naturally prepared the romantics to discover and impose certain principles which today are still proudly referred to by the surrealists.]

This is as concise and as lucid an explanation of the surrealists' debt to late eighteenth- and early nineteenth-century writers as can be found.

In the second category of artists who oppose society there are the creators of the absurd, and Alfred Jarry, creator of *Ubu Roi,* is mentioned as a prime example of this reaction. Tzara praises Jarry for having:

. . . consciemment sorti l'humour d'une certaine bassesse crapuleuse, en lui donnant sa signification poétique. Créateur aussi de *l'inattendu* et de *la surprise.* Magnifique manieur de *l'absurde* et de *l'arbitraire.*[25]

[. . . consciously taken humor away from a certain filthy lowness, by giving it its poetic significance. Creator also of

the *unexpected* and of the *surprise*. Magnificent handler of
the *absurd* and the *arbitrary*.]

Jarry is perhaps even more important as a precursor of
dadaism than of surrealism, and, in this respect, mention
should be made of the varying attitudes of dadaism, surrealism, and existentialism to the absurd. The dadaist
revels in the absurd, the surrealist uses and studies it,
while the existentialist attempts to form an authentic
existence after the recognition of life's absurdity.

There are also writers who form a third category, those
who renounce literature and take personal refuge elsewhere. Gérard de Nerval and Arthur Rimbaud are given
as the best examples of this. In fact both of them, through
their *lives*, reflect the evolution of modern poetry. What
Tzara means by this is that they both began by writing
quite intelligible poetry (political poetry in Nerval's case)
and finally ended up by showing "la tendance de trans-
poser la poésie dans la vie quotidienne, tendance qui in-
consciemment impliquait que la poésie *pouvait exister en
dehors* du poème." [26] [the tendency to transpose poetry
into daily life, a tendency which unconsciously implied
that poetry *could exist aside* from the poem.]

Finally, we may classify some of Tzara's poetic precursors of surrealism as "language destroyers." The first
of these are the "Bousingots." Petrus Borel and Charles Lassailly, nineteenth-century poets, find favor for having
pointed out the incapacity of words to utter sentiments.

Indeed, it is significant to note that the only poetic quotations in the entire "Essay on the Situation of Poetry" come from Borel and Lassailly. The first quotation, "Hop! hop! hop!" is from the former. The second quotation, which makes as much sense as the first, is from Lassailly:

<pre>
                    Ah!
          Eh!   he?
     Hi!   hi!   hi!
Hu!   hu!   hu!   hu!   hu! 27
</pre>

Lautréamont and Apollinaire are both praised by Tzara for their personal destruction of linguistic conventions, Lautréamont for having created a sort of verbal magic in which reason is subverted and logic defeated,[28] and Apollinaire for his experimentation in poetry and for suppressing punctuation in his poems. When punctuation, the servant of logic and order, was abolished, poetry could become something other than the ordered expression of rational thought. Tzara also extols the technique of the *Calligrammes* and points out a parallel between them and the dada use of collage and the commonplace. The use of the commonplace and collage illustrates the dada conviction that *tout se vaut* (everything is worthwhile) or, perhaps more precisely, that *rien ne vaut* (nothing is worthwhile). Certainly the abject misery of language was demonstrated by dada.

Si Dada n'a pas pu se dérober au langage, il a bien constaté les malaises que celui-ci causait et les entraves qu'il mettait à la libération de la poésie. La désorganisation, la désorientation, la démoralisation de toutes les valeurs admises étaient pour nous tous d'indiscutables directives. Le dégoût devint un dogme et la spontanéité un principe moteur.[29]

[If Dada wasn't able to escape language, it clearly pointed out the sicknesses caused by language and the hindrances language put in the way of the liberation of poetry. The disorganization, the disorientation, the demoralization of all accepted values were unquestionable commands for us. Disgust became a dogma and spontaneity a driving principle.]

Tzara ends his backward glance at dada as precursor of surrealism on a sad note. "Je conçois fort bien aujourd'hui que les espoirs de certains d'entre nous à l'égard de Dada aient été déçus. Dada avait trop promis et la Révolution ne venait pas." [30] [Today I understand perfectly that the hopes of some of us with regard to Dada were disappointed. Dada had promised too much and the Revolution didn't come.] Tzara had no way of knowing that the same epitaph would in a short time be appropriate for surrealism.

Throughout his "Essai sur la Situation de la Poésie," Tzara's growing belief in Marxism is expressed. He declares that: "La poésie pourrait devenir un *élément de vie* —au même titre que le rêve—mais ce passage ne saurait s'effectuer sans celui de l'individu au collectif." [31] [Poetry could become a *life element*—in the same way as dreams—but this change couldn't be effected without that of the individual to the collective.] The last three words show that indeed surrealism could be put in the service of the revolution, and that the revolution in question is largely political and economic. Tzara insists that all "directed" thought is in the service of the bourgeoisie and that the few authentic practitioners of poetry as "activité de l'esprit"—Nerval, Sade, Lautréamont, Rimbaud, etc.—illustrate a common and violent opposition to this dominating class. For Tzara, the real history of modern poetry has been the attempt by certain poets to change poetry from a means of expression in the hire of the bourgeoisie to a free mental state. He expresses the conviction that social revolution must accompany this artistic revolution to bring about the poetry of the future.

> Si dans la société actuelle la poésie constitue un refuge, une *opposition* à la classe dominante, la bourgeoisie, dans la société future où l'antagonisme économique des classes disparaîtra, la poésie ne sera plus soumise aux mêmes conditions.[32]

> [If poetry in the present society constitutes a refuge, an *opposition* to the dominant class, the bourgeoisie, in the society of the future when the economic antagonisms of the classes disappear, poetry will no longer be subjected to the same conditions.]

Tzara even claimed that "non-directed" thought could flower in a communist society, liberating man from long working hours.

> Par quel moyen empêchera-t-on ce qui sera le travail pro-
> ductif de ressembler à ce que nous sommes habitués d'appeler
> la paresse et le loisir de devenir virtuellement le travail?
> L'activité poétique est seule capable de donner là une con-
> clusion humaine de libération. Il faut organiser le rêve, la
> paresse, le loisir, en vue de la société communiste, c'est la tâche
> la plus actuelle de la poésie.[33]

> [How will the productive work of the future be prevented
> from resembling what we are used to calling idleness, and
> leisure from becoming to all intents and purposes work? Poetic
> activity alone is able to furnish here a human conclusion of
> liberation. We have to organize dream, idleness, leisure, with
> a view to communist society; this currently is the task of
> poetry.]

Tzara very definitely links communist revolution with the attainment of a new and surrealistic life. This attitude is slightly different from that expressed four years later by André Breton.

> I will never tire of contrasting with the imperious current
> need, which is to change the much too shaky and out-of-date
> social foundations of the old world, that other not less im-
> perious need, which is not to view the coming Revolution as

an end. . . . The end for me can only be in the knowledge
of man's eternal destiny.[34]

Breton (unlike Tzara) stresses *knowing* as much as *changing*. The latter clearly defines his own goal in the conclusion to the "Essay on the Situation of Poetry."

Tendre; de toutes ses forces; à l'accomplissement de la Révolution, en poursuivant parallèlement l'activité poétique qui se
justifie du point de vue du matérialisme dialectique, voilà,
me semble-t-il, le rôle historique du Surréalisme: organiser le
loisir dans la société future, donner un contenu à la paresse
en préparant sur des bases scientifiques la réalisation des im-
menses possibilités que contient la phrase de Lautréamont:

"La Poésie Doit Etre Faite Par Tous. Non Par Un." [35]

[To adhere with all its energies to the accomplishment of the
Revolution, while at the same time pursuing the poetic activity
which justifies itself from the point of view of dialectical
materialism, this, it seems to me, is the historic role of surrealism, to organize leisure in the society of the future, to
give a content to idleness by preparing on scientific founda-
tions the realization of the immense possibilities contained in
Lautréamont's phrase:

"Poetry Should Be Made By All. Not By One."]

How does this essay relate to other surrealist criticism
and in particular to that of André Breton? Tzara's attack

on "poetry-means of expression" obviously separates him from Breton. Although in his manifestoes Breton calls for everyone to "practice" poetry, he does not turn his back on those whose practice has been in writing.[36] The fact that Breton calls Dante, Shakespeare, Chateaubriand, Victor Hugo, Mallarmé, Marceline Desbordes-Valmore, and Saint-John Perse surrealists shows that he in no way rejects "poésie-moyen d'expression." If Breton was not in agreement with Tzara about "poésie-moyen d'expression," he did agree that poetry could at times be a common unifying experience. Breton even asserted that:

> The characteristic of surrealism is to have proclaimed the total equality of all normal human beings before the subliminal message and to have constantly asserted that this message constitutes a common patrimony of which it rests entirely with each person to claim his own share and which at all costs should very soon cease being considered as the prerogative of a few.[37]

This movement toward making art a collective human experience is prepared by what Tzara calls "poetry as state of mind." His distinction between this new concept of poetry and the traditional concept has been taken up by other surrealists—for example, by Jules Monnerot in his article on "Poésie comme Genre et Poésie comme Fonction," and by Paul Eluard in his collection of verse entitled *Poésie Involontaire et Poésie Intentionelle*.[38] In all cases, the author is proposing "non-directed" thought which is directly communicable as a substitute for the techniques of verse writing. Tzara, however, parts company with others who share this interest in mental liberation (such as Breton and Eluard) when he categorically attacks the traditional concept of poetry as art form.

With the "Essai sur La Situation de la Poésie," Tzara has taken a new direction. His journey from dada to surrealism is understandable and perhaps inevitable. He has attempted in the essay to evaluate the meaning of modern poetry as movement toward communal expression. This lucid article, one of the key texts for an understanding of certain basic forces underlying dadaism and surrealism, shows that Tzara has matured, that some of his dadaist combativeness has given way to a serious attempt to understand and explain the meaning of the surrealist adventure. Four years later, Tzara will elaborate these ideas in *Grains et Issues*.[39]

Figure 14. Tzarra, Vieille Liqueur, Théodore Fraenkel, n.d. ("rectified" advertisement for a nearly undrinkable Basque liqueur). Reproduced from *Revue de l'Association pour l'Étude du Mouvement Dada,* no. 1, p. 47 (October 1965).

4 *Grains et Issues*

Grains et Issues, which appeared in 1935, is a curious combination of prose statements and poetry. It also contains several rather long critical notes which set forth artistic theories held by Tzara at this time. The main subjects in the book are the function of dreams, the relation between social and linguistic revolution, and considerations on metaphor and the function of poetry. One of the most original aspects of this work is the introduction of what Tzara called "experimental dreams." In the "Essay on the Situation of Poetry," he had already mentioned his indebtedness to Gérard de Nerval for whom dream was a "second life," and the dream was, of course, a central surrealist concern. Breton had given evidence of the importance he attached to oneiric experience in the *Surrealist Manifestoes.* Perhaps the most successful surrealist practitioner of dream literature was the poet Robert Desnos, who, so it was claimed, could very easily enter a trance-like state and subsequently relate the content of his subliminal visions.

Tzara adds a new type of revery to the surrealist repertory: the "experimental dream." The former mathematics student, continuing to be enchanted with the scientific, wished to give his writings the trappings of serious investigation in this domain. In a note on "Le Rêve Expérimental," Tzara describes this newest of the genres and its inception.

C'est la première phrase: "A partir de ce jour . . ." qui m'a fourni l'idée de rapporter à la réalité sensible les faits matériels que j'y inventais au fur et à mesure le long de mon travail. Mais c'est dans cette invention même qu'apparut le piège de l'élément lyrique, non conforme à la réalité environnante ou supposée possible, qui devait jouer un rôle décisif dans l'élaboration de ce conte.[1]

[It's the first sentence: "From this day on . . ." that gave me the idea of relating the material facts that I invented progressively throughout my work to tangible reality. However, there appeared in that invention the snare of a lyrical element which was not in conformity with the surrounding or supposedly possible reality, and which was to play a decisive role in the elaboration of this story.]

What Tzara calls the "lyrical element" is the product of the subconscious, and this becomes a decisive factor in the new genre. Tzara's originality lies in the invention of a literary form in which there is a continual give and take between "directed" thought and its "undirected" counterpart. The encroachment of the irrational on a logical succession of facts has an unsettling effect on the reader. One begins *Grains et Issues* with a comforting feeling of *déjà vu,* but footing is suddenly lost as this "lyrical element" washes away meaning, or, as Tzara puts it, "déborde du récipient" [overflows its receptacle], until one is once again deposited on the familiar shores of reason. This feeling of strangeness is, however, the result of traditional mental habits. In Tzara's mind, the rational and the "lyrical" are not opposed but are interdependent "structure and superstructure." [2] They co-exist even if at times the "lyrical" threatens to destroy the rational, "l'anéantir dans son essence" [to destroy it in its essence]. [3] Tzara, in his definition of dream, points out that it is not a quantitative fact but a qualitative "zone" which contributes to the intelligibility, the "prise de conscience" of certain phenomena.

> Le rêve est qualité d'un mouvement psychique donné, d'un dégagement de forces qui, sous l'action d'un levier pour l'instant inconnu, est capable de faire passer d'un état à l'autre certains phénomènes en vue d'une synthèse qui est un acte de connaissance, qui est quantité et que nous désignons sous le nom de poésie. [4]

> [Dream is a quality of a given psychic movement, of a release of forces which, responding to the action of an as yet

unknown compulsion, is capable of causing certain phenomena to pass from one state of being to another in the direction of a synthesis which is a quantitative act of knowledge and which we call poetry.]

Poetry is thus no longer the glorification of objective reality, but rather its decomposition and rearrangement by the constructive force of the subconscious. It is the point at which the limits between dream and reality will no longer exist, in short, the realization of the unity sought after by the surrealists "of those two states which in appearance are so contradictory, dream and reality, in a sort of absolute reality, a *surreality. . . .*" [5] Tzara is implementing Breton's program through the intervention of the "lyrical" (or "non-directed") activity in the rational domain, explaining that this intervention is produced by the wish to "éclaircir le problème de l'interpénétration des mondes rationnel et irrationnel." [6] [to explain the problem of the interpenetration of the rational and irrational worlds.] In studying the relationship between poetry and dream, he decries the fact that all too often there is a simple equation between the two. He criticizes over-zealous surrealists who claimed that both poetry and dream are simply pure automatic responses to stimuli. With his customary throughness and his penchant for cultural anthropology, Tzara states that one must go back to primitive man to discover the real essence of poetry and dream. This is necessary because "nondirected" thought was very important in primitive cultures and dreams did not constitute the forbidden domain which they do in the twentieth century. Dream was a means of knowledge and not merely a receptacle for repressed desires. For Tzara, a great and unfortunate change had taken place since the time of primitive man, when one lived a "poetic" and "dream-filled" life. This psychic change has its social counterpart and "ce renversement de valeurs coïncide avec la transformation des sociétés collectivistes en sociétés individualistes" [7] [this overturning of values coincides with the transformation of collectivist societies into individualist societies].

After having cautioned against assuming a too narrow relationship between poetry and dream, Tzara proposes certain definitions of their respective functions. He first mentions dreams.

. . . le symbole *onirique* se concentrant en un point sur une ligne donnée par la limite entre le conscient et l'inconscient, *tire* sa substance des faits refoulés de la profondeur du subconscient, de leur masse, en les faisant converger vers ce point dont le processus d'éclosion en pleine conscience . . . constitue le symbole perceptible. . . .[8]

[. . . the *oneiric* symbol, centering itself in a point on a line formed by the boundary between the conscious and the unconscious, *draws* its substance from the mass of repressed facts in the depths of the subconscious by making these facts converge toward that point whose process of birth into full consciousness . . . constitutes the perceptible symbol. . . .]

The *poetic* symbol has a quite different action, although its genesis is the same.

> . . . le symbole *poétique,* prenant naissance sur la même frontière et figuré aussi par un point (qui serait le processus de sa prise de conscience à travers les images, les métaphores, etc.) projette sur le monde extérieur, par divergence et sous une forme supérieure, des faits correspondants à ceux qui gisent à l'état latent sur les fonds du monde intérieur.[9]

> [. . . the *poetic* symbol, having been born at the same junction and also represented by a point (which would be the process of its grasp of consciousness through images, metaphors, etc.) projects on an exterior world through divergence and in a superior form facts corresponding to those which lie in a latent state in the depths of the inner world.]

Thus the poetic action is an externalization whereas the dream exerts an inner pull. "Le rêve et la poésie seraient, sur des plans différents, le même pivot autour duquel les refoulements arriveraient à être objectivés"[10] [Dream and poetry would, on different levels, be the same pivot around which inhibitions would come to be brought to the surface]. It is reasonable to assert that poetry can have a therapeutic effect on the poet, but it is more difficult to accept Tzara's efforts to ". . . établir dans quelle mesure l'état psychique où se plonge le poéte . . . répond à un fort désir de retour *intra-maternel*"[11] [. . . establish in what measure the psychic state into which the poet plunges himself responds to a strong desire for an *intra-maternal* return]. Using Freudian jargon, Tzara says that the creation of a poetic paradise is a sublimation, the creation or recapture of "pre-natal comfort." The appro-priation of Marxist and Freudian jargon by Tzara is of course often disturbing and has not gone unnoticed by such critics as Gaston Derycke, who protests: "Oui, tics, que ce recours au primarisme prétentieux de nos intel-lectuels marxistes, que cette utilisation maniaque d'un jargon freudien. . . ." [12] [Yes, tics, this return to a pre-tentious elementalism of our Marxist intellectuals, this in-sane use of Freudian jargon. . . .].

What is Tzara's contribution to the surrealist concept of the dream? The obvious answer is that he enriched this concept by insisting that dream and reality could *coin-cide* in a most creative form of poetry. [13] His efforts were to serve the surrealist cause by elevating the dream, through references to experimentation, Hegelian change, and cultural anthropology, to the status of an indis-pensable solvent which would dissolve the normal way of interpreting reality. In this sense, his remarks on dream help to promote the surrealists' goal which was the libera-tion of man, and they deserve to be considered along with other documents, such as Breton's *Trajectoire du Rêve*, [14] as one of the most interesting, if difficult and jargon-ridden, elucidations of this central surrealist theory.

Figure 15. The constructivist-dadaist congress in Weimar, 1922. Originally published in L. Moholy-Nagy, *Vision in Motion.* Courtesy Sibyl Moholy-Nagy.

The second major consideration in *Grains et Issues* is the relationship between social and linguistic revolution. Tzara had made brief mention of this idea earlier in his "Essay on the Situation of Poetry," but it was not fully developed until the later work. For Tzara, all art should, like society, be in perpetual change, for it is closely linked with economic and social processes.[15] For poetry to enter into daily life as a *function* and not as an art form, the entire social structure must be completely changed, as must the supporting linguistic framework.

> Que les événements sociaux jouent un rôle de premier plan dans ces changements, que le langage lui-même soit un phénomène d'ordre social, rien de plus incontestable quand on pense à de multiples exemples fournis par l'histoire des langages et celle des mots.[16]

> [When you think of the multiple examples provided by the history of languages and of words, there is nothing more incontrovertible than the notion that social events play a primary role in these changes and that language itself is a phenomenon of a social order.]

The inventor of the "experimental dream" says that for language to become a really useful tool which could resolve man's inner conflicts, the outward structure of society would have to be changed. "Semantic anarchy" [17] is not an adequate solution. Indeed, there cannot be any satisfactory solution until the current oppressors have been thrown down.

> C'est donc au changement de la société actuelle, à la suppression radicale de la classe oppressive . . . qu'est liée l'intégration correcte, c'est-à-dire en correspondance avec le langage, dans le monde, de nouvelles données de la science sans laquelle nous perdrons bientôt tout contact avec ce qui nous entoure et sans quoi nous ne saurions vivre en conformité avec nous-même.[18]

> [Thus it is to the changing of present society and to the radical suppression of the oppressive class . . . that is linked the correct integration, in connection with language, in the world, of new scientific principles without which we would soon lose all contact with our surroundings and would not be able to live in conformity with ourselves.]

These then are general principles: Society must be changed as must language in order for man to remain healthy in a rapidly changing world. Tzara's specific recommendations for linguistic change are found in his remarks on metaphor and the function of poetry. In the nineteenth century one of the poetic war cries was "War on rhetoric but peace toward syntax."[19] Tzara goes much further than Victor Hugo by calling for a transformation of syntax, the necessary concomitant to a repudiation of logic.

> L'expression de la pensée devra être impudique, insolente et brutale, même injuste à la rigueur, si elle ne veut sombrer

dans l'annulation verbale qui, au degré de nos connaissances actuelles, doit être considérée comme improductive et tauto-logique.[20]

[The expression of thought will have to be immodest, insolent, brutal, and, if need be, unjust if it is not to fall into verbal annulment which, given the degree of our current knowledge, must be considered as being unproductive and tautological.]

One could argue that the efforts of Mallarmé constitute what Tzara would call an "annulation verbale" or, in Mallarmé's own words, an "aboli bibelot d'inanités sonores" [abolished bibelot of sounding inanity]. For Tzara, words should break down meaning by an accumulation of their own weight. Tzara chooses accumulation rather than "annulation," or Rimbaud over Mallarmé.

Linguistic and social evolution seems agonizingly slow to Tzara because it is held back by the nefarious bonds of common sense and reason. Tzara continued to play the role of "anti-honnête homme," the man who could never love reason by asserting that

. . . la paresse intellectuelle, par une étrange ironie dénomme le *bon* sens quand c'est le *mauvais* qu'il aurait dû s'appeler, la routine, la force inerte de l'habitude et les résistances qu'elles opposent aux méthodes de connaissance et d'investi-gation.[21]

[. . . intellectual laziness, by a strange irony speaks of *good* sense when it ought to be called *bad* sense, routine, dull force of habit and resistance to means of knowledge and investigation.]

In the place of this sluggishness, Tzara would substitute a new way of thinking: by metaphor. This frees thought by breaking down the traditional rigidity of simple identification between sign and object. Faithful to a dialectical approach, he describes thought process as essentially comparison, this comparison leading to a synthesis which will occur during a true poetic state. Moreover, thinking by metaphor is not simply confined to poets but exists in a latent form in all of us. Tzara, like Lautréamont, believes that poetry should be made by everyone and that we should accept a new way of thinking which would bypass words. The images produced by this "non-directed" way of thinking would, like everything else, be in constant motion.

> La thérapeutique . . . consisterait donc à apprendre . . . à passer d'une chose à l'autre selon le mode métaphorique (ce passage excluant par son dynamisme même toute idée de pessimisme organique), c'est-à-dire: l'emploi naturel et continu du transfert dans le processus de réduction et de dissolution de toute image du monde dont le malade a pris connaissance et qu'il a inhibée, ou, si l'on veut, d'une manière plus générale: une méthode de systématiser l'oubli. . . .[22]

> [The therapy . . . would thus consist in learning to move from one thing to another according to the metaphorical mode (this movement excluding by its very dynamism any idea

of organic pessimism), that is to say, the natural and con-
tinuous use of transfer in the process of reduction and dissolution of any image of the world which the patient has
become conscious of and which he has inhibited, or if you
wish, in a more general manner, a method of systematizing
forgetfulness. . . .]

To paraphrase Apollinaire, "To whom shall we owe the
forgetting of a continent?", Tzara wishes for us to forget
and to sabotage, to "traduire en une réalité tragique, en
une réalité qui ne vous laisse pas de répit, brusque et
émouvante, mais non pas sujette à des manières bassement
descriptives, la réalité manifeste du monde sensible." [23] [to
express in a tragic reality, in a reality which leaves you no
respite, blunt and moving, but not subject to basely descriptive manners, the manifest reality of the tangible
world.] This is an excellent description of the surrealist
enterprise. It has always been the goal of Tristan Tzara
and in fact the goal of true surrealist poetry because as
Tzara says:

Toutes les facultés disponibles en vue de saboter la réalité du
monde extérieur et ses inacceptables manifestations et de les
atteindre dans le noyau même de leurs aboutissants de misère
. . . convergent déjà vers le foyer de cet agencement de la
transparence des choses et des êtres, la poésie.[24]

[All the faculties available for sabotaging the reality of the
exterior world with its unacceptable manifestations, and for
striking them down at the very core of their miserable cir-

cumstances . . . are already converging on the center of that arrangement of the transparence of things and beings which is poetry.]

Dreams and poetry were "les principes actifs" for Tzara during his five-year association with surrealism. What is the importance of his critical foray into this realm? [25] The "Essay on the Situation of Poetry" remains as one of the most complete studies of a social orientation found in the poetic precursors of surrealism. This essay also contains the elaboration of Tzara's definition of "poésie-activité de l'esprit" and "poésie-moyen d'expression." His appropriation of Jung's terminology is felicitous in supporting this interpretation of modern French poetry and is significant in that it underlined a certain transition from the concept of the individual artist to that of art as collective vision. Tzara was thus able to make a considerable contribution to the definition of surrealism, but he could not stay within its confines. His inability to remain a surrealist is understandable, given the fact that surrealism was to become for many a literary movement rather than the revolution it had set out to be.[26] Tzara was a surrealist until late 1935, which was a turning point for him. At this time, in a speech before the Congrès International des Ecrivains, he openly declared himself a communist. Most of the surrealists eventually chose between art and revolution, surrealism and communism; these last two, at times unified in aim, became progressively more incompatible.

An excellent critic, A. Roland de Renéville, sums up their basic differences:

> While the surrealists meant to liberate man through the analysis of his inner nature and devoted themselves to an idealistic idea of reality, the communists, on the other hand, followed Karl Marx by opting for a materialist interpretation of the world and aimed at integrating the individual into a rigorous social order where individual initiatives would find themselves commanded by the interest of the collectivity.[27]

From the ideas on art elaborated in the "Essay on the Situation of Poetry" and *Grains et Issues*, Tzara would move to a more marked political involvement. *Grains et Issues* was his last testament as a more or less orthodox surrealist.

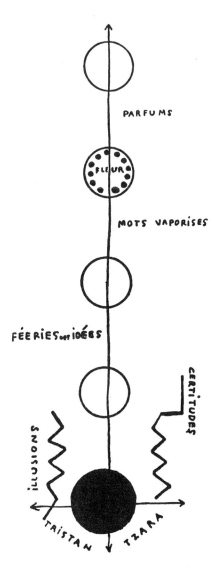

Figure 16. Portrait of Tristan Tzara, Francis Picabia, 1920 (ink drawing). Originally published in *Cannibale,* no. 1, April 25, 1920. Reproduced from Michel Sanouillet, *Francis Picabia et 391,* vol. 2, p. 183 (Paris: Eric Losfeld, 1966).

5 "Initiés et Précurseurs" and *Inquisitions*

The year 1935 marks not only the publication of *Grains et Issues* but also Tzara's turning away from the aesthetic or surrealist revolt to political revolution. This final disenchantment with Breton's group is first documented in a letter to *Les Cahiers du Sud* explaining his refusal to contribute to the surrealist magazine *Minotaure*. In his letter, Tzara insists that the theories set forth in "L'Essai sur la Situation de la Poésie" were his personal ideas and were not to be taken as the expression of surrealist doctrine, which he now repudiated. He also asserts that:

> La conclusion qu'il aurait importé de tirer non seulement de mon "essai," mais de l'attitude même du surréalisme à l'égard de la poésie, serait celle que le problème de la poésie, tel qu'il est posé actuellement en connexion avec l'action révolutionnaire, dépasse largement les cadres d'un groupement

hétérogène qui, basé sur un minimum d'entente de ses membres, concrétise une activité d'ordre *pratique* et se situe par là-même hors du débat.[1]

[The conclusion which should have been drawn, not only from my essay but from the very attitude of surrealism with regard to poetry, would be that the problem of poetry as it is now posed in connection with revolutionary action, goes well beyond the frame of a heterogeneous grouping which, based on a minimum of understanding among its members, puts into concrete form an activity of a *practical* order and thus places itself outside of the question.]

Tzara particularly decries the attempt to make poetry an end in itself.

Une récente tentative de quelques surréalistes, de constituer un "front commun" de la poésie dans une revue parisienne, à laquelle René Char et moi avons refusé de collaborer, tentative confusionelle que je réprouve violemment, démontre que la poésie est considérée par eux comme *un but en soi*, ce contre quoi, en raison même de l'affectation révolutionnaire de celle-ci, je ne saurais jamais assez m'élever.[2]

[A recent attempt by a few surrealists to set up a "common front" in poetry in a Parisian review in which René Char and I have refused to collaborate—a confusion-producing attempt which I disapprove of violently—demonstrates that poetry is considered by them as *a goal in itself*. Because of the revolutionary nature of poetry I cannot protest enough against such a position.]

The second pronouncement which confirms Tzara's rejection of surrealism is his speech, "Initiés et Précurseurs," given before the Congrès International des Ecrivains pour la Défense de la Culture in June of 1935 and printed in the July issue of *Commune*. This congress was organized by the communist group L'Association des Ecrivains et Artistes Révolutionnaires. Its importance is evident from the list of participants, which included André Gide, E. M. Forster, Aldous Huxley, Boris Pasternak, and André Malraux. It is obvious that all these people were not loyal party members at the time, but the meeting was nevertheless presented under communist auspices. Tzara spoke to this group more as a "precursor" than as an "initiate." He was not on the editorial board of *Commune*, the voice of the "AEAR," nor was he a member of the organizing committee for the meeting. His Marxist leanings had been expressed in "L'Essai sur la Situation de la Poésie," but he was now for the first time accepted as a comrade. This is borne out by the editorial comment in the July, 1935 issue of *Commune*.

> We wanted to join here the addresses by Tzara and by Chamson because they mark two steps forward by two extremely different writers: Tzara, the founder of dadaism comes out in favor of poetry rejecting its tawdry finery to blend into life, that is to say into Revolution.[3]

This comment is absurd in a sense because Tzara had been saying nothing else since 1916. From the first dada manifesto on, we have seen that Tzara has called for poetry to "blend with life." The new development here is that with the speech "Initiés et Précurseurs," Tzara has finally accepted communism as the only valid revolutionary force. It must be remembered, however, that at this time Tzara was not speaking as a member of the group. His poetry had shown nothing which would cause him to be esteemed by the party leaders, and, as we have seen from the seven *Dada Manifestoes,* his earlier revolutionary pronouncements were completely undisciplined and anarchical. In this speech, Tzara not only urges strict adherence to the *one* revolution, but he also attempts to defend undescriptive, hermetic poetry, and to rationalize its worth as a revolutionary instrument. This was indeed a difficult task. Quoting a stanza from a typical poem printed in an earlier issue of *Commune* might make Tzara's difficult position more understandable. It seems to be the type of poetry which the editors considered most effective.

Il avait travaillé au Turksib
Dans la 7ième brigade de choc de Koula.
Et parce qu'il gueulait toujours
Et trouvait du temps pour maudire des brebis galeuses,
Il fut envoyé dans un kolkhoze
Au Caucase.

C'était un géant.
Il buvait parfois et battait sa femme souvent
Parce qu'elle ne comprenait rien au communisme.

Mais dans ses vieux jours,
Alors que les vieux bolcheviks étaient morts
Il citait par ordre alphabétique, prénoms en tête,
Tous les héros d'octobre dix-sept
Sans en excepter un.[4]

[He had worked in Turksib in the 7th Koula Shock Brigade.
And because he was always shouting and always found time
to curse the black sheep, he was sent to a collective farm in
the Caucasus.

He was a giant. Sometimes he drank and often he beat his wife
because she didn't understand anything about communism.
But in his aging days, when all the old Bolsheviks were dead,
he cited in alphabetical order, first names first, all the heroes of
October 17 without missing a single one.]

This poem is completely unlike Tzara's less explicitly revolutionary work. Tzara wished to make clear his im-
patience with "poetry as means of expression" even if
this poetry was in the service of Marxism.

Combien de fois n'a-t-on pas entendu dire que, puisque
les poètes se déclaraient révolutionnaires, ceci devait être
visible dans leurs œuvres? C'était là le résultat d'un de ces pro-
cédés de simplification qui ont souvent déformé des discussions en mettant de la passion dans les débats sans issue.
C'était prendre la poésie pour ce qu'elle avait vraiment été
à certains moments de l'Histoire, pour un moyen d'expression,
un peu plus puéril que les autres. . . .[5]

[How many times haven't we heard that since poets declare themselves to be revolutionaries this ought to be evident in their works? This attitude was the result of one of those simplifying processes which have frequently twisted discussions by introducing emotion into debates leading nowhere. It was to take poetry for what it had been at certain historical moments, for a means of expression slightly more puerile than the others. . . .]

Tzara's constant effort was to *expand* the limits of poetry, making poetry something other than a mere literary exercise. His effort is at once an attempt to discredit poetry and to invest it with vast new possibilities. Tzara does not write about communal farms and workers' living conditions, because he does not write about *anything* at all. Poetry is no longer description. It is exploration and pure creation.

Sans qu'elle soit exprimée, la poésie peut encore de nos jours être décelée dans les mœurs, dans la vie quotidienne, dans les activités les plus prosaïques, car, allant de l'emploi des cartes illustrées aux panneaux publicitaires, de la persistance des lieux-communs aux inventions de la mode féminine, elle rejoint cette autre faculté humaine, fondamentale, puisque impliquée dans la formation de la pensée et du langage: le don de la métaphore.[6]

[At the present time, poetry, without being expressed, can still be found in customs, in daily life, and in the most prosaic activities, because, going from the use of illustrated cards to that of advertising signboards, from the persistence of commonplaces to the inventions of feminine fashions, poetry rejoins that other human faculty which is fundamental because it is implied in the formation of thought and of language: the gift of metaphor.]

Tzara had already expressed himself on the importance of metaphor in *Grains et Issues*. The mention of "inventions de la mode féminine" invites a parenthesis here, a reference to Tzara's article which appeared in *Minotaure*, before he publicly renounced that luxurious surrealist magazine in 1935. The article is entitled "D'un certain automatisme du goût." "Poetry" in feminine fashions, according to the article, seems to reside in their expression of certain deep-seated psychological tendencies.

Les chapeaux des femmes me font redécouvrir le temps où l'invraisemblable invasion des fleurs m'apportait, avec la fraîcheur de la jeunesse et de la désolation, le sens d'une volupté tactile et visionnaire que je dus regarder comme la confirmation de ma nature sous sa forme la plus secrète, celle des représentations sexuelles.[7]

[Women's hats cause me to rediscover the time when the unbelievable invasion of flowers would bring me, along with the freshness of youth and grief, the sense of a visionary and tactile voluptuousness which I must have interpreted as the confirmation of my nature in its most secret form, that of sexual representations.]

This Freudian foray into *la mode* is accompanied by an incredible number of photographs by Tzara's friend, the American dadaist-surrealist, Man Ray, all illustrating this imaginative thesis. Besides women's hats, modern architecture is mentioned as being potentially capable of supplying this "poetry" by returning to man what has been ravished from him during childhood and adolescence, namely "le clair-obscur des profondeurs tactiles et molles" [the chiaroscuro of soft and tactile depths] which reproduce the happy prenatal state. Tzara calls for circular, irregular, and spherical houses which could reflect this condition. "L'Architecture de l'avenir sera intra-utérine . . . si elle renonce à son rôle d'interprète—serviteur de la bourgeoisie dont la volonté coercitive ne peut que séparer l'homme des chemins de sa destinée." [8] [The architecture of the future will be intrauterine . . . if it renounces its role as interpreter-servant of the bourgeoisie whose coercive will can only separate man from the paths of his destiny.] With his customary assurance, and, in view of the non-intrauterine accomplishments of such architects as Mies van der Rohe, with rather poor judgment, Tzara asserts: "L'architecture 'moderne' aussi hygiénique et dépouillée d'ornements qu'elle veuille paraître, n'a aucune chance de vivre." [9] ["Modern" architecture, however hygienic and bare of ornament it wishes to be, has no chance of surviving.] This parenthetical reference to Tzara's article in *Minotaure* actually points up the constant effort on his part to widen the definition of poetry.

The conviction that poetry is *independent* of language was again a main point in his 1935 speech at the meeting for the defense of culture. Let us return to that speech.

After explaining his own idea of "poetry as a state of mind," Tzara traces its evolution, repeating his remarks in "L'Essai sur la Situation de la Poésie" and reiterating points made in *Grains et Issues* about the relationship of the poetic and social revolutions. The real significance of this speech with respect to Tzara's personal development is his increased interest in sociology.

> . . . la poésie a trait à la science des rapports entre les hommes, la sociologie d'une part et, d'autre part, aux formes combatives qu'a prise la volonté des hommes de se libérer des contraintes sociales.[10]

> [. . . poetry is connected to the science of relationships between people, to sociology on one hand, and, on the other, to the combative forms which the will of men has taken in order to liberate itself from social constraints.]

However, Tzara expresses the idea that what seems even more important to him than poetry, which after all is only a literary product, is the situation of the *poet* with respect to society.[11] He had essayed a definition of the situation of poetry in *Le Surréalisme au Service de la Révolution;* now, speaking before the "AEAR," he attempts to define the situation of *the poet*. Tzara's question is: What is a poet? The answer for him is that a poet

". . . représente un élément de continuelle révolte, de
turbulence, et par conséquent, une force capable de
remuer les couches profondes de la pensée humaine." [12]
[. . . represents an element of continual revolt, of turbulence, and as a consequence, a force capable of stirring up
the deepest layers of human thought.] Thus the poet is a
rebel by definition, but if this is so, what form should his
revolt take? Can abstract poetry like Tzara's own possibly
serve the revolution? And if so, how?

Ainsi, actuellement, la poésie ne peut être une fin en soi,
quelque chose comme la poésie pour la poésie, mais un moyen
propre au poète d'accéder à la conscience révolutionnaire.
Malgré l'apparence hermétique de la poésie, malgré cette
algèbre personnelle formée de processus de symbolisation qui,
pour être traduite, nécessite une sorte d'initiation, elle-même
liée à la rencontre de certains caractères psychiques, il s'agit
d'une poésie faite *pour* l'homme et non pas d'un homme
fait *pour* la poésie. Il s'agit d'une poésie qui pourrait abandonner les oripeaux des mots et des images pour se confondre avec la révolution. [13]

[Thus, at the present time, poetry cannot be an end in
itself, something like poetry for poetry's sake, but a means
suited to the poet in order to comply with revolutionary
consciousness. Despite the hermetic appearance of poetry,
despite that personal algebra formed from the process of
symbolization, which to be translated needs a sort of initiation, itself linked to the encounter of certain psychic char-

acteristics, it is a question of a poetry created *for* man and
not of man created *for* poetry. It's a question of a poetry
which could abandon the tinsel of words and images to
merge with revolution.]

Tzara is clearly placing the work of art on a lower scale
than the man behind the work and the men for whom
it is intended. He is also saying that even the most abstract poetry can serve the revolution. "S'il s'agit non pas
d'interpréter le monde, mais de le changer, personne n'a
prétendu qu'il ne faille le connaître et le comprendre,
car cette connaissance même du monde implique la nécessité de son changement." [14] [If it is not a matter of interpreting the world but of changing it, no one has maintained that it isn't necessary to know and understand it
because that very knowledge of the world implies the
need for its transformation.] Sartre says almost the same
thing in *Qu'est-ce que la littérature?* when he states that
the simple fact of naming a thing is also an appeal to
change it. He terms this "action by disclosure." Tzara's
thesis is that poetry is a source of knowledge, and that this
knowledge will show change to be necessary.

Through his earlier writings we have seen how Tzara
recoils from poetry as celebration or cradle-song. In this
speech he has a few words to say about bliss in poetry.
"Il n'est pas possible dans la misère actuelle . . . que la
poésie exprime autre chose que le désespoir." [15] [In the
present state of misery it isn't possible . . . for poetry

to express anything but despair.] His audience knew that, in speaking of "la misère actuelle," Tzara was referring to the events in Spain and the spreading menace of fascism in Europe which had caused the poet to turn away from the exterior world and to exhibit

> . . . un esprit particulier de caste, où, le dégoût de la classe possédante, accompagné de l'impossibilité de s'assimiler à la classe des dépossédés, et le refus de prendre comme un point d'appui le monde extérieur, refus résultant d'un trop fort désir de s'y intégrer totalement, ont engendré un état latent de fureur et de haine . . ." [16]

> [. . . a private clannish turn of mind, where disgust of the ruling class accompanied by the impossibility of assimilating oneself in the class of the dispossessed, and the refusal to take as a frame of reference the exterior world, this refusal resulting from a too strong wish to integrate oneself totally, have engendered a latent state of fury and hatred. . . .]

Tzara claims that although this pessimistic refusal is the mood best suited to the events of the day, there is room for hope if the poet would realize that "la plus élevée valeur poétique est celle qui coïncide . . . avec la révolution prolétarienne." [17] [the most elevated poetic value is that which coincides . . . with the proletarian revolution.] For Tzara, this is the only basis for optimism. He is no longer the exponent of a dadaist, anarcho-revolutionary protest. He has made his decision.

Tzara's withdrawal from surrealism is reconfirmed by his participation in an abortive attempt to form a "surrationalist" movement including not only poets and painters but also scientists and philosophers. This group would continue the attack on reason more systematically than the surrealists, and they would apply themselves to a much wider range of questions. The sole testament of the surrationalists appeared in early 1936. It was the one issue of a review entitled *Inquisitions* which was purported to be the "Organe du Groupe d'études pour la Phénoménologie Humaine." The directors of this review were Louis Aragon, Roger Caillois, J. M. Monnerot, and Tzara. The main contributors were the above and Gaston Bachelard, the philosopher and literary critic; Jacques Spitz, whose article on the quantum theory in physics illustrates how close some of the avant-garde poets were to new directions in scientific investigation; and René Crevel, whose article was published posthumously.

A close study of this unusual publication is rewarding with respect to an insight into Tzara in at least three ways. First, the bitter attack on surrealism printed within its covers shows a rejection of the surrealist movement, which must have been shared by editor Tzara. Second, the inclusion of material related to Heisenberg and other physicists illustrates, as previously mentioned, the scientific bent of some of the former surrealists, including Tzara. Finally, Tzara himself contributed two articles to this review, one, "Le Poète dans la Société," showing the continuation of the sociological approach which he had called for in "Initiés et Précurseurs," and the other, "De la Nécessité en Poésie," adding new ideas on poetic function and bringing Tzara's critical judgment to bear on such contemporary poets as Blaise Cendrars, L.-P. Fargue, Paul Claudel, and Paul Eluard.

The best introduction to the common purpose which held together these various intellectuals is furnished by a speech delivered by Tzara before a meeting of the group for La Phénoménologie Humaine on the eighth of January, 1936, and printed in *Inquisitions*. Tzara explains that what brought this heterogeneous group together was the conviction that certain intellectual problems should not be considered exclusively with regard to literature. Nearly all the surrealists were writers or painters, but the surrationalists wished to merge different disciplines in the hope of seeing

> . . . l'homme à sa place naturelle, ou de l'y remettre pour que ses activités le servent et ne le rejettent plus dans sa solitude tragique. . . . Pour cette raison . . . nous nous plaçons délibérément sur le plan que veut et doit créer le Front Populaire tel qu'il l'a déjà créé sur le terrain de la pratique politique. C'est dire que nous n'entendons poursuivre nos recherches dans un monde extérieur à celui qui nous définit *socialement*.[18]

> [. . . man in his natural place, or restoring him to that place so that his activities serve him and no longer fling him into a tragic solitude. . . . For this reason . . . we deliber-

ately place ourselves in sympathy with the program that the Popular Front wishes and must create, such as it has already created in the realm of practical politics. This means that we do not intend to pursue our researches in a world other than that which defines us *socially*.]

Mention of "Le Front Populaire" leaves no doubt as to Tzara's political sentiments. In another *Inquisitions* article, Louis Aragon is equally explicit. ". . . it goes without saying that for my part, my position is taken, and from that experience in my opinion nothing can be valuable except that which can be put into the context of Marxism." [19]

One might protest to Tzara and Aragon that surrealism too is a revolution and that the surrealist poets are leaders of subversion. The answer given to this by Pierre Robin, another member of the *Inquisitions* group, is probably little different from the reply Tzara himself would have made. Robin chooses a lecture by Salvador Dali for his remarks, but the same general criticism could be leveled at any of the surrealists whose *champ d'action* remained entirely in the arts.

The subversive aspect which appears in the social type of the buffoon only exists in appearance: the king whom only the buffoon can make fun of with impunity, knows full well that the jeering takes place on an imaginary plane, in a fictitious world which the king, at any moment, if he so wishes, can abolish, and which exists only because of his complicity. He derives from this just the right dose of masochistic satisfaction and an appreciable aesthetic enjoyment in seeing his power and position trampled underfoot—without having that position and power really put in jeopardy.[20]

The inquisitors not only hunt down those who are occupied only with aesthetics, they also try to seek out and expose reason itself. Gaston Bachelard speaks for the group on this point, deriding the poverty of the empirical approach. He assails reason, saying that it is usually nothing but dreary recourse to certitudes of memory. He wishes to turn reason upside down, having more interest in the future than in the past and more enthusiasm for experimentation than for memory. He calls for an "experimental reason" which would parallel Tzara's "experimental dream" in order to bring about "sur-empiricisms of a strange, innovating force." [21] Bachelard also mentions some implications of the *scientific* developments of the time, which by challenging established tenets were an encouragement for the poets to question purely traditional aesthetic theories. The scientific dogma to receive the most criticism was determinism. The orthodox view in physics was that one could positively *determine* the trajectory of an electron if one knew its speed and position, whereas the new quantum theory showed that one could not know both speed and position at the same time. The new idea of indeterminacy [22] was seized by the surrationalists as an example of the unpredictable in the physical world and as a dramatic illustration of the breakdown of the old concepts.

The same temper of challenge shows in Tzara's main contribution to *Inquisitions,* "Le Poète dans la Société," where he first expresses his satisfaction at seeing such literary critics as Roger Caillois and Jules Monnerot attack the traditional privilege of poetry. "Le mystère dont on l'entoure, volontairement ou non, contribue à la hausser sur le plan sentimental à un niveau d'autant plus élevé que la raillerie dont elle est l'objet à la base se fait sentir sous une forme plus agressive." [23] [The mystery with which it is surrounded, voluntarily or not, plays a part in raising it on the sentimental level to a degree all the more elevated as the railling of which it is a basic object makes itself felt in a more aggressive form.] Poetry, as Tzara says repeatedly, is a way of thought and not simply a form of descriptive literature.[24] His concern is with situating the poetic function among the other forms of human endeavor in a changing world.

> Elle [la poésie] est un passage. Elle tend à s'intégrer dans la vie, en abandonnant sa forme. Les transformations qu'a subies la forme à travers les siècles m'incitent à penser que d'autres transformations . . . peuvent aller jusqu'à la perte de ses caractères perceptibles.[25]

> [It (poetry) is a passage. It tends to integrate itself into life by abandoning its form. The transformations which its form has undergone throughout the centuries lead me to believe that other changes . . . can go so far as to make it lose its perceptible characteristics.]

The mention of final transformations which will completely alter the character of poetry is probably the result of Tzara's continued application of Hegel's theory of change to aesthetics. It confirms the poet's belief in the necessary dissociation between the former rigid poetic norms and the true poetic art. "C'est dans la sphère généralisée de la pensée humaine qu'il faudra situer les manifestations de la poésie." [26] [It is in the generalized sphere of human thought that the manifestations of poetry should be situated.]

His second article for *Inquisitions* Tzara entitles "De la Nécessité en Poésie." He expresses an almost Platonic belief in the poetic necessity or, perhaps more justly, revolutionary *fury*. For Tzara, the poet is not one who has the intention of writing in verse. He is a man seized by the imperious need to express an imaginative vision of the world. This powerful grip of "poésie-activité de l'esprit," according to Tzara, has loosened since the Renaissance.

A partir de la Pléiade, où certaines influences de la poésie populaire du moyen-âge se font encore sentir, le rappel de la poésie latine aidant, la poésie-activité de l'esprit perd de plus en plus sa vigueur, tandis que le moyen d'expression prend une importance plus grande. Racine serait à considérer comme situé à mi-chemin de cette évolution.[27]

[Since the Pléiade in which certain influences of the popular poetry of the Middle Ages still made themselves felt, remembrances of Latin poetry also contributing, poetry as mental activity progressively loses its vigor, while poetry as means of expression takes on a greater importance. Racine should be considered as being a half-way point in this evolution.]

Isolated poets would attempt to redress the balance before dada and surrealism would offer their help. After these basic considerations of the poetic act, Tzara gives a criticism of a recently published anthology of poetry. He shows interest in Blaise Cendrars and Léon-Paul Fargue, saying that their effort was to reduce poetry from the esoteric to the commonplace. Both Cendrars and Fargue use a conversational tone at times which, in Tzara's opinion, helps to subvert Poetry with a capital P in favor of something more human and easily shared by everyone. Tzara also sees in these two poets an attitude he believes to be necessary in all great poets, that of aggressiveness, of *lycanthropie*.[28] Tzara explains *lycanthropie* and its relationship to the poetic act in the following manner:

> La déterminante lycanthropique est, pour ainsi dire, souterraine, elle est présente uniquement dans une impulsion qui reste invisible pendant la durée du poème. Aussi, la part de penser non dirigé y est plus grande. . . . Le mot comme signification tend lui-même à disparaître sous la pression de la houle que provoque le mouvement puissant de la poésie-activité de l'esprit.[29]

[The "lycanthropic" determinant is, so to speak, subterranean. It is present only in an impulse which remains invisible during the life of the poem. Thus the portion of non-

directed thought is greater in it. . . . The word as signification itself tends to disappear under the pressure of the surge
provoked by the powerful movement of poetry as mental
activity.]

One of the most interesting aspects of this article is
that Tzara is forced to speak of Paul Claudel's poetry.
His remarks about Claudel show that despite his *parti
pris*, Tzara could not fail to admire the poetry of a man
who also felt the ". . . pression de la houle que provoque
le mouvement puissant de la poésie-activité de l'esprit."
It is, of course, a difficult task to fit Paul Claudel, *Ambassadeur de France*, into Tzara's definition of the poet as
a rebel. How this champion of social stability and adherence to what Tzara felt was a repressive capitalistic society could "aller de pair avec une révolte et une turbulence des plus productives, ceci ne s'explique pas aisé-
ment." [30] [go along with the most productive revolt and
turbulence, isn't easily explained.] Moreover, Claudel had
become the *bête noire* of the surrealists by asserting that
the only significant thing about the dadaists and surrealists
was that they were all pederasts.[31] The surrealists replied
in their now famous *Lettre Ouverte à M. Paul Claudel,
Ambassadeur de France au Japon*, saying among other
things:

> Peu nous importe la création. Nous souhaitons, de toutes
> nos forces, que les révolutions, les guerres et les insurrections

coloniales viennent anéantir cette civilisation occidentale dont vous défendez jusqu'en Orient la vermine et nous appelons cette destruction comme l'état de choses le moins inacceptable pour l'esprit.

Il ne saurait y avoir pour nous ni équilibre ni grand art. Voici déjà longtemps que l'idée de beauté s'est rassise. Il ne reste debout qu'une idée morale, à savoir par exemple qu'on ne peut pas être à la fois ambassadeur de France et poète.[32]

[Creation matters little to us. We deeply hope that revolutions, wars, and colonial insurrections will annihilate this Western civilization whose vermin you defend even in the Orient, and we call upon this destruction as the least inacceptable state of affairs for the mind.

There can be for us neither equilibrium nor great art. For a long time now the idea of beauty has been settled. There is only moral idea remaining, to know for example if one can be at the same time Ambassador of France and a poet.]

The fact that Tzara openly declares that Claudel *is* indeed a great poet is all the more interesting when one realizes that Louis Aragon, a signer of the letter to Claudel, was a director of the *Inquisitions* group. Tzara has always been less willing than many of his *confrères* to have his mind made up for him. He tries to explain the Claudel enigma in speaking of ". . . la transposition de ce monde en un autre meilleur . . . selon la religion, après la mort."[33] [. . . the transposition of this world into another better one . . . according to religion, after death.] Tzara asserts that this violent opposition to the society in which one lives could be explained in Claudel's case by the desire for a better existence in the afterlife.

> Prisonnières d'un ordre social à base dominatrice et répressive, comment les représentations de révolte arrivent-elles à se sublimer dans une figuration antithétique, voilà le problème que pose, à côté du mode d'existence de P. Claudel, sa poésie et, par là même, la déformation des idées religieuses mises au service du conservatisme bourgeois.[34]

> [Prisoners as they are of a social order which is fundamentally dominating and repressive, how can the representations of revolt succeed in refining themselves into an antithetic figuration? This is the problem posed, aside from the way of life of P. Claudel, by his poetry and, by this very fact, the deformation of religious ideas put in the service of bourgeois conservatism.]

Other poets mentioned as having more consciously identified themselves with the revolution are Desnos, Eluard, Michaux, and Péret. Tzara calls them ". . . l'élément progressif par lequel la poésie poursuit sa rapide évolution par bonds sur la trajectoire montante de la poésie-activité de l'esprit."[35] [. . . the progressive element by which poetry follows in leaps and bounds its rapid evolution on the ascending trajectory of poetry as activity of the mind.]

The study of "Initiés et Précurseurs" and of Tzara's contributions to *Inquisitions* has shown how he drew away from surrealism in the thirties. The passage from surrealism to surrationalism for Tzara was a passage from aesthetic dream to positive action, from psychological and aesthetic to sociological considerations. Without altering the fundamental concepts upon which his artistic theories were based, but by changing the stress in certain areas, Tzara's revolt has become more precise and it is now human progress which holds his attention. The bitter first-hand experience of the Spanish Civil War and of World War II and life under the occupation would confirm him in his belief that involvement in aesthetic matters is much less important than vigorous social action. His role in both proved the sincerity of his beliefs.[36]

« L'art est mort, libérons notre vie quotidienne. »
Sorbonne graffito, May 1968

PART THREE

Postsurrealism

6 Critical Perspectives

Among Tzara's published postwar critical opinions, those on Henri Rousseau,[1] Tristan Corbière,[2] Pablo Picasso,[3] and Arthur Rimbaud[4] are the most significant, although he has studied François Villon,[5] René Crevel,[6] Pierre Reverdy,[7] Paul Eluard,[8] Guillaume Apollinaire,[9] and others.

Tzara's preface to Henri Rousseau's two plays, *Une Visite à l'Exposition de 1899*, and *La Vengeance d'une Orpheline Russe*, appeared in 1947. These plays could not have failed to interest Tzara, since there are several techniques which are common to both the theatre of Rousseau and that of Tzara. By studying Tzara's remarks on these works, particularly those on *Une Visite à l'Exposition de 1899*, one is able to obtain an insight into Tzara's own thoughts on theatre and on art in general.

The principal ideas expressed in Tzara's introduction center around the example of Rousseau as a "complete artist," on the concepts of space and time as embodied in Rousseau's theatre, and finally on "le merveilleux involontaire" of Le Douanier. In speaking of the "complete artist," Tzara asserts that:

> Le type de *l'homme omniscient* que la Renaissance avait mis en avant comme le parfait représentant de l'humanisme rationaliste et encyclopédique de ce temps, a trouvé dans *l'artiste complet* un équivalent dont la tradition populaire a gardé jusqu'à nos jours le souvenir.[10]

> [The symbol of *omniscient man* which the Renaissance had put forward as the perfect representative of the rationalistic and encyclopedic humanism of its period found in the *complete artist* an equivalent of which popular tradition has to this day retained the memory.]

Tzara had long held that the way of expressing oneself was in itself unimportant. Since art was not merely a means of expression but rather a state of mind, the true artist could express himself in any or in several media. Rousseau, of course, serves Tzara's purpose here very well because in addition to being a painter and playwright he was also an accomplished musician and a poet. It might be said that many artists have a "violon d'Ingres," but the point is that Rousseau treated all his artistic means of expression as equally important. He played his violin as seriously as he painted.

Rousseau is also important, in Tzara's opinion, for the

significant ways in which he differs from the romantics and from the surrealists. For Tzara, Rousseau is an artist who refuses to accept any romantic and mystical ideas about artistic inspiration. There is a denial on his part of "l'importance exagérée donnée à l'inspiration telle que les romantiques l'envisageaient comme une grâce supra-terrestre, véritable communion avec on ne sait quel pou-voir mystérieux." [11] ["the exaggerated importance given to inspiration as the romantics conceived it as a supra-terrestrial grace and veritable communion with who knows what mysterious power.] Rousseau's work also serves to illustrate a refusal of surrealism. Tzara had com-pletely abandoned surrealism by this time and he uses Rousseau to discredit certain surrealist postures.

A la question: le tableau est-il une réalité par lui-même ou sert-il à représenter une réalité imaginée, certains peintres surréalistes ont répondu en optant pour la seconde propo-sition. Cette réaction contre une peinture ayant sa propre fin dans ses moyens adéquats risque de devenir à son tour . . . l'expression d'un intellectualisme obscurcissant. De toute évi-dence, ce choix engendre de nouveaux poncifs qui sont en train de s'édifier sur les ruines de l'académisme traditionnel.[12]

[To the question: is the painting a reality in itself or does it serve to represent an imagined reality, certain surrealist paint-ers answered by opting for the second proposition. This reac-tion against painting that has its goal in its own means, risks becoming in its turn . . . the expression of a confusion-producing intellectualism. It is obvious that this choice engenders new conventionalisms which are building on the ruins of traditional academism.]

Tzara had for some time pleaded that art should be founded in lived experience and not simply be the product of the imagination. He sees Rousseau as a healthy exponent of the literal in painting. While many painters attempt to reduce the anecdote to the minimum, Rousseau always considered the *subject* as the center of his preoccupations.[13] Tzara had said in *Inquisitions* that he no longer believed that art could have a purely aesthetic goal.[14] If indeed the work must have another goal, which in Tzara's case is to speak to the inner man and to speed the liberation of man and mind, then the anecdote cannot be completely abandoned. The totally abstract work risks non-communication.

Rousseau's handling of space and time is also of interest to Tzara. The almost complete disrespect found in Rousseau's plays for what is often normal treatment of time and space has influenced other avant-garde artists and is evident in Tzara's *Le Mouchoir de Nuages,* which is an early surrealist-type play.[15] Tzara mentions the cinematographic qualities in Rousseau's theatre, the rapid succession of scenes, and the epic scale of the stage—at one point Rousseau calls for two homes, several villas, and the Neva flowing in the background. This simultaneous technique reminds Tzara of other "primitive" painters and of Breughel. In a very apt metaphor, Tzara asserts that, in order to accept Rousseau's vision, our intelligence must function like a ladder rather than a stairway, suppressing all that is unnecessary.[16] An American critic, Roger Shattuck, confirms Tzara's interpretation.

> When Rousseau scatters through a landscape several figures identical in size and shape, when he paints the figures of *Les Joueurs de Football* so much alike that we can easily see the same man in four successive positions (and even these positions broken down into separate parts), and when he fills his tropical canvases so full of detail that it can only be taken in a little at a time as the eye moves across the surface—in all these cases he suggests the possibility of an unrolling in time as well as in space. It is cinematographic time (a succession of "stills"), not chronological time.[17]

An example of this crowding of images in time and space by Rousseau is shown in *Une Visite à l'Exposition* by the record time in which the peasant family "does" Paris. They seem literally to fly from one place to another. Tzara calls this an effort to "synthesize movement." "Cette synthétisation qui, sous certains aspects, fait prévoir le découpage cinématographique détermine, entre autres, le caractère *moderne* de son œuvre."[18] [This synthesizing which, in certain ways anticipates cinematographic cutting is responsible for, among other things, the *modern* character of his work.] This effort to break down the bonds of time and space is consistent with Tzara's

Figure 17. Les joueurs de football, Henri Rousseau, 1908 (oil on canvas). Courtesy Solomon R. Guggenheim Museum, N.Y.

description of the artists as "lycanthrope" and revolutionary and derives from what Tzara would term a necessary and forceful will to change man's position in the world.

However, if the general order of the world is to be changed, things, ordinary objects, will themselves remain and are indeed worthy of being described in artistic works. Tzara's perceptive remarks about Rousseau show that the ex-dadaist anticipates the tentatives of the "chosistes" and the American "Junk School" of art. The question remains whether a work should simply represent an imaginary reality. Tzara and Rousseau both say no.

> Rousseau a été un précurseur dans ce début du siècle où les promesses de la mécanisation vont de pair avec la découverte de la poésie dans l'actualité de l'objet usuel. De la lampe à pétrole de Rousseau à la guitare, au journal, aux cartes à jouer et au paquet de tabac de Picasso, de Braque et de Gris, le chemin, à travers "l'esprit nouveau" d'Apollinaire (et plus tard de Léger) passe par la "Tour Eiffel" de Delaunay et ses "fenêtres" pour aboutir au Futurisme.[19]

> [Rousseau was a precursor in the early years of a century when the promises of mechanization are accompanied by the discovery of poetry in the reality of the everyday object. From Rousseau's kerosene lamp to the guitar, the newspaper, the playing cards, and the tobacco pack of Picasso, Braque, and Gris, the path through Apollinaire's (and later Léger's) "esprit nouveau" passes through Delaunay's "Eiffel Tower" and "windows" and ends up in Futurism.]

Moreover, Tzara could have pointed out that this cult of the everyday object did not stop with the futurists. It was an integral part of dada with Picabia's spark plugs, Schwitters' rags and tatters, and Duchamp's "readymades." This cult still flourishes today with such painters as the American, Robert Rauschenberg, who creates with stuffed animals, old dirty beds, light bulbs, Coca-Cola bottles, and automobile tires. Tzara's article on Rousseau is important for its description of the birth of this trend in art.

> Dans les premiers pas de ce modernisme naissant, on décèle la tendresse pour l'objet familier, humble objet de tous les jours, l'objet pris dans sa totalité virtuelle et plastique. L'objet sujet des cubistes contient implicitement une charge affective qui l'accompagne, lui sert de support et constitue en somme son commentaire poétique.[20]

> [In the first steps of this infant modernism, one can discern a tenderness for the familiar, humble, everyday object, the object taken in its virtual and plastic totality. The object-subject of the cubists implicitly contains an accompanying affective charge which serves it as a support and makes up its poetic commentary.]

Tzara describes Henri Rousseau as being a person who, sensing the overwhelming complexity of the world, combats this complexity simply by denying it. He constructs a private world in which complexity becomes reduced to the accumulation of details. Rousseau's handling, his distortion rather, of space and time is a reaction to this problem of complexity. Tzara perhaps best describes this reaction which he finds in Rousseau in another article called "Le Fantastique comme déformation du temps." [21]

> Mais toute stabilité n'est elle-même qu'un moment imperceptible, aussi faut-il croire qu'à l'apparence d'une hypertrophie sensorielle il sera aisé d'opposer efficacement sans suppression de détails, la précipitation cinétique et rotative d'images d'un monde accéléré.[22]

> [However, all stability is in itself only an imperceptible moment. Thus one is led to believe that in contrast to the appearance of a sensory hypertrophy it would be easy to set up effectively and without suppression of details, the cinematic and rotating precipitation of an accelerated world.]

Thus, the production of fantastic art and Rousseau's treatment of space and time both seem to satisfy what Tzara called for in the dada manifestoes: " . . . the whirlwind . . . a tottering world in flight, betrothed to the glockenspiel of hell . . . riding on hiccups." [23]

Tzara praises Rousseau's ability to see things as children and primitives see them, an ability which can be found in ". . . les couches profondes des âges de l'humanité. Là tout est jeu, calme et volupté. La liberté d'interpréter édéniquement le monde est réservée à ceux pour qui l'enfance a grandi sans abandonner sa pureté primordiale." [24]

[. . . the deep strata of the ages of humanity. There, all is play, calm, and voluptuousness. The freedom to interpret the world in a Paradisiac manner is reserved for those whose childhood progressed without a loss of primordial purity.] This of course had been said before, notably by Baudelaire, who claimed that genius was childhood recaptured at will. Tzara's substitution of "jeu" for Baudelaire's "luxe" is felicitous, though, for one cannot overlook Le Douanier's sense of humor.

What is more important, however, is that Rousseau's style is "a style of life"; the man *is* the work. Rousseau is the total artist whose art consists in his way of confronting the world. Tzara is always curious about what impels an artist to sense and express a conception of the world at variance with what we might call a realistic vision. He believes that a partial solution to this puzzle may be found in a study of the mental process of the mentally deranged, the child, and the savage. By what means could one explore these depths?

. . . il est évident que tout état échappant au contrôle direct de la perception par les moyens d'objets appartenant au milieu—le rêve, les narcoses, pourra nous faire prolonger ou écourter la vie et qu'il n'est pas exclu que de nouvelles méthodes puissent encore être mises au service des explorations de la conscience, en tout état d'éveil, soit par des interventions physiologiques dans la structure optique de l'organisme sensoriel, soit par des exercices intellectuels capables d'assouplir la volonté en endormant justement ces facultés de l'intelligence, raides et bourrues, qui nous dirigent dans la vie selon des règles schématiques.[25]

[. . . it is obvious that any state which escapes the direct control of perception through the means of objects belonging to the surroundings—dream, drugs, can lengthen or shorten the experience of life, and it isn't out of the question that new methods may yet be put in the service of exploration of the consciousness, in a wide-awake state, either by physiological interventions in the optical structure of the sensory organism, or by intellectual exercises capable of loosening up the will by putting to sleep those stiff and churlish faculties of the intelligence which run our lives according to schematic rules.]

Tzara believes that Henri Rousseau was an illustration of a kind of mentality which would have to be explored by the methods described. He also believes that Le Douanier's work is an honest expression of a mind not unlike that of a primitive. It is evident that Tzara takes Rousseau very seriously, seeing in him the embodiment of a priceless state of mind toward which all art should tend.

Il nous confirme dans l'idée que des surprises sont réservées à ceux qui . . . trouvent comme Rousseau, leur justification profonde, dans une liberté s'accommodant de l'espoir qui leur est encore accordé, ne serait-ce que sur le plan de l'esprit et malgré les conditions provisoires ou misérables du monde actuel, de l'espoir en une harmonie ample et

fraternelle dont de nombreux Douaniers sont toujours prêts
à défendre la pureté aux frontières du possible.[26]

[He confirms us in the belief that surprises are reserved
for those who . . . find their profound justification, like
Rousseau, in a freedom which makes the best of a hope which
is still granted them, even if this hope is only in the sphere
of the mind and despite the provisional or miserable conditions in the world today—of a hope for an ample and fra-
ternal harmony whose purity numerous Douaniers are always
ready to defend at the frontiers of the possible.]

Tristan Corbière would certainly belong to this category of artists who expose "the provisional or miserable
conditions in the world." In 1950, Tzara wrote an important preface to an edition of *Les Amours Jaunes*.[27]
This preface also appeared in *Europe* in December of the
same year.[28] Tzara considers Corbière an excellent example of a strong artistic compulsion to speak out and
of the frustration caused when words themselves prevent
complete self-expression. He is also interested in Corbière's
use of a verbal collage technique and in the fact that Corbière is a poet of revolt. Part of this revolt is aesthetic
and is found in the elliptical style and unpolished immediacy of many of Corbière's poems, a style and immediacy which appealed to Tzara. Albert Sonnenfeld, in
his excellent study, agrees with Tzara that Corbière
represents a revolt in poetry, calling his work "a treason
against poetic tradition" and an example of "anti-

Figure 18. Self-portrait, Tristan Corbière, n.d. (medium unknown). Reproduced from Jean Rousselot, *Tristan Corbière*, p. 29 (Paris: Seghers, Poètes d'Aujourd'hui, 1951).

poetry."²⁹ For Tzara, the treason and revolt found in *Les Amours Jaunes* come from an overriding need to cry out, which precludes any niceties of form. This desire to speak out leads Tzara to reflect on the poetic vocation.

Tout en étant, par ailleurs, naturelle à chaque individu, par quel étrange processus revêt-elle chez quelques êtres privilégiés le caractère d'une abnégation totale, d'un don à une cause qui n'est que leur propre vie et qui, cependant, remue autour d'elle des vies parallèles, de lourdes couches de mémoire, d'intraduisibles aspirations vers des libertés à peine pressenties?³⁰

[While being at the same time natural to each individual, by what strange process does it, in the case of a few privileged beings, take on the character of total abnegation, a gift to a cause which is simply their own life and yet which stirs parallel lives, awakening heavy strata of memory, untranslatable aspirations to as yet scarcely imagined freedoms?]

There are three important points to make about this "privileged being," the artist. The first is that the artistic process, according to Tzara, requires a total abnegation. Tzara means that one must attempt to lay bare the core of one's being, and that this must be done totally with no limitation imposed by the exterior personality. Second, the expression "stirs parallel lives, awakening heavy strata of memory . . ." means that the artist must express certain common, though generally unvoiced, sentiments. He must express Jung's "collective unconscious." Poetic greatness can be measured by its universality.[31] Finally, Tzara claims that the creative urge is present in all of us. This article on Corbière is an excellent illustration of Tzara's criticism. He first chooses his subject carefully, and then treats not only the man in question and his work, but takes advantage of the article as a pretext for general considerations on the evolution of modern art. By so doing, he explains and justifies a significant part of modern art including his own work. Tzara is always most concerned with situating the subject with respect to the movement he discerns in art toward total liberation from formal concerns. His articles on pre-Columbian and Oceanic art, as well as his studies of certain individual artists, reveal an almost geological interest in getting down to the underlying psychic substratum on which the modern mentality rests. Solitude is a part of this substratum which Tzara finds in several modern artists, and particularly in Corbière.

> Ce Solitaire parmi les solitaires vit dans un monde violemment communicatif où les imprécations et les évocations lui tiennent lieu de compagnons et de témoins. Il est dans la nature de ceux qui luttent pour garder intact leur isolement de ne voir en celui-ci que le dépit d'un trop grand amour des hommes, une impossible communion sur le plan des échanges affectifs.[32]

> [This solitary being out of all solitary beings lives in a violently communicative world where imprecations and evocations take the place of companions and witnesses. It is in

the nature of those who struggle to keep their isolation intact to see in it only the resentment of a too great love for
people and an impossible communion in the area of affective
exchanges.]

Corbière is an example of the artist who, wishing to enter
into a dialogue with others, and finding this dialogue
prevented, experiences bitter anguish.[33]

Les mots ne lui semblaient plus que des instruments déri-
soires ou criminels. Mais lui-même, qui découvrait partout
des signes demeurés purs, chez les peuples primitifs et dans
le folklore, n'y aurait évidemment jamais pensé s'il n'avait
d'abord aimé les hommes pour eux-mêmes, qui n'ont dans
leurs manifestations populaires rien d'autre qu'eux-mêmes à
livrer.[34]

[Words no longer seemed to him anything more than deri-
sory or criminal instruments. But Corbière himself, who
everywhere discovered signs which remained pure in primitive
cultures and in folklore, would obviously never have thought
about it if he hadn't first loved people for themselves, people
who in their popular expressions have nothing but themselves to give.]

Tzara, who, like Baudelaire or Apollinaire, is a poet interested in painting, calls Corbière "le plus peintre des
poètes," stressing his use of "verbal superpositions."[35] In
speaking of Corbière's painterly turn, Tzara might have
mentioned the fact that several Parisian painters made

Corbière's town, Roscoff, their summer headquarters. Corbière spent much time with these artists and once remarked after seeing one of the artists' painting of sheep:

> You do them less well than Charles Jacques, who does them less well than Troyon, who did them less well than nature. One should not paint what one sees. One should only paint what one hasn't and will never see.[36]

Tzara would not always agree with this statement of aesthetic principle as much as would André Breton, who included Corbière's "Litanie du Sommeil" in his *Anthologie de l'humour Noir* as an early example of automatic writing.[37]

The "verbal superpositions" mentioned by Tzara as being important in Corbière's poetry anticipate the collage technique in painting. This technique always interested Tzara, and its use by Corbière brings him close to Apollinaire and Picasso, giving further unity to Tzara's critical proclivities. These "superpositions" are made up of everyday sayings, apostrophes and snatches of conversation. This effort to make poetry out of the commonplace or, perhaps, and more precisely, to change the level of poetry to that of everyday experience, makes Corbière an ancestor of the dadaists.

One of the central ideas in Tzara's concept of poetry is revolt. He has described contumacy as a necessary attitude for the poet. Its abundant presence in the life and work of Tristan Corbière, according to Tzara, may stem in part from Corbière's ambivalent attitude toward his father. Tzara remarks that Corbière was torn between a strong admiration for his father and an equally strong disgust with him. The disgust came when Tristan found that his father's swashbuckling sea stories were the products of a keen imagination rather than personal experience. These statements by Tzara are significant, since it is Corbière's revolt that links him strongly with Rimbaud and gives further cohesion to Tzara's criticism. Tzara finds that both of these poets were in search of moral absolutes in a world where such absolutes were lacking. Rimbaud's reaction to Charleville and Tristan Corbière's reaction to his father, Edouard, was to create an imaginary and marvelous world of escape. Both poets try by verbal means to destroy a mediocre existence. Corbière's invective, however, often ends in a strangled gasp.

> L'impossibilité de crier, au moyen des mots, la faute du père, celle du monde . . . Le cri, ultime expression de l'homme traqué par sa propre insuffisance, le cri étranglé dans la gorge, le cri, ressort réduit à l'impuissance, et cependant unique possibilité de se manifester quand la raison et le sens des choses ont cessé d'agir utilement—quand la beauté, et la laideur elles-mêmes perdent leurs droits à l'existence—le cri devient alors une protestation sans réplique et l'affirmation d'une vérité implacable, définitive.[38]

> [The impossibility of crying out through the use of words the father's fault and that of the world. . . . The shriek,

final expression of man run to earth by his own insufficiency, the shriek strangled in the throat, the shriek, resort made impotent, and nonetheless the only possibility for asserting oneself when reason and the meaning of things have ceased to act usefully—when beauty and ugliness have themselves lost their right to existence—the shriek then becomes an un-answered protest and the affirmation of an implacable and definitive truth.]

This is a brilliant poetic appreciation of Tristan Corbière. Tzara insists that the cry cannot be feigned as it was by some romantic poets, and he also insists that crying out, trying to reach out to others, is fraught with many dangers. In struggling for fraternity and knowledge, the poet risks his own spiritual death.[39]

Another poet who fought for knowledge and faced solitude was Lautréamont. Tzara finds similarities in the basic psychological attitude of Lautréamont and Corbière. Both poets shared an ambivalent attitude toward humanity, and both, seeing justice sullied, found comfort in the anonymous forces of nature.[40] Besides asserting that Corbière's revolt stemmed in part from his attitude toward his father, Tzara remarks that Corbière manifests the social revolt of the bourgeois artist who repudiates the class in which he was born.

En se déclassant, Corbière non seulement a tenu à rendre manifeste son mépris à l'égard de ses pairs, mais au moyen des exagérations et des mystifications à créer autour de lui cette zone de silence, de crainte respectueuse et cette distance dont le poète a besoin pour faire coïncider la teneur de sa vie avec le sens de sa poésie. Ne pourrait-on pas avancer que le principe mobile des poètes appelés "maudits" consiste dans la tendance à unir leur vie et leur poésie en l'unique expression d'une réalité ambivalente? [41]

[By coming down in the world, Corbière not only wished to manifest his scorn for his peers, but through use of exaggeration and mystification he wished to create a zone of silence around himself, a respectful fear and that distance needed by the poet in order to make the tenor of his life coincide with the meaning of his poetry. Couldn't one contend that the driving principle of so-called "damned poets" consists in the tendency to unite their life and their poetry in the single expression of an ambivalent reality?]

For Tzara, a poet's life and work must be consistent. The bourgeois artist like Corbière finds liberty through opposition to his class and withdrawal from it. But one might ask: "What kind of liberty is this? Can liberty exist in a void?" Tzara replies that the poet's liberty requires a confrontation with the reader's liberty.[42] To sustain a life of freedom, a climate of freedom must be present. In Tzara's opinion, this usually takes the form of a clan or a small coterie of artists, such as that of the dadaists, in which the individual artists can buoy each other up in their opposition to a despised society. Tzara interprets the relationship between Corbière and his painter friends as a continuation of the clannishness of the "Jeunes-France" and "Bousingots."

Although Tzara speaks of the general social revolt of Corbière, he is forced to admit that Corbière had no specific political ideas. He is also disconcerted by the abundance of punctuation found in Corbière's poetry. Despite this, Tzara maintains that any quarrel with Corbière's form of expression should not take anything away from the admiration due the man and from the general importance of his work. Tzara's article lucidly situates Tristan Corbière in the movement from "Les Bousingots" through Rimbaud and Lautréamont to Apollinaire. Tzara's remarks on love, "verbal exasperation," aesthetic and social revolt with respect to Corbière are illuminating and helpful in adding to the ever-increasing reputation of one of France's important lyric poets.

It has been mentioned that Tzara always had an interest in painting. He associated with such painters as Jean Arp, Francis Picabia, and Marcel Janco from the days of the Cabaret Voltaire and he contributed articles on art to *Les Cahiers d'Art* and wrote introductions to books by artists. Perhaps Tzara's most significant relationship with art was through his personal friend, Pablo Picasso. Tzara's most important critical appreciation of Picasso is his article, "Picasso et les Chemins de la Connaissance." [43] He also wrote a brief "Présentation d'une exposition de papiers collés de Picasso." [44]

In "Picasso et les Chemins de la Connaissance," Tzara succinctly explains his critical approach.

Figure 19. Pablo Picasso and Tristan Tzara at Vallauris in 1950.
Reproduced from René Lacôte and Georges Haldas, *Tristan Tzara*, p.
128 (Paris: Seghers, Poètes d'Aujourd'hui, 1952). Photo L. Prejger.

Mon propos n'est pas d'expliquer la peinture de Picasso, mais de la faire insérer dans un ensemble de relations adéquates à l'esprit du temps. La compréhension fine de la peinture ne s'acquiert que dans la mesure où le spectateur éprouve la conscience d'un cheminement de la pensée et de la sensation plus ou moins semblable à celui que le peintre a laissé derrière lui.[45]

[My purpose is not to explain Picasso's work but to fit it into a set of relationships corresponding to the temper of the times. Expert understanding of painting is acquired only in the measure to which the viewer experiences a progression of thought and feeling which is more or less similar to that which the painter himself experienced.]

Tzara's concern is always to situate an artist with respect to a period or with respect to a certain broad movement of ideas. There are several reasons for Tzara's admiration for Picasso. Surely one of the most important is the common political persuasion of the two men. Another is the fact that Picasso represents, for Tzara, an evolution which parallels that of the poets whom Tzara most respects.

One of Tzara's most famous dictums was "thought is made in the mouth"; he can say with respect to Picasso: "thought is made with the hand," meaning that in Picasso's work there is a very close connection between the thought and its expression. Tzara, of course, appreciates those works that transcribe "non-directed" thought with no reference to rational analysis. The work must be captured at its moment of inception and it must also have its roots in a search for knowledge. The title of this article becomes clear when one realizes that Tzara conceives the artist as one whose principal motivation is a desire *to know*. Tzara's concept is particularly applicable to Picasso, when one considers the myriad explorations presented in the painter's work. The concept of art as *jouissance* is replaced by Tzara with a concept of art as *connaissance*. Tzara asserts that this search for comprehension, which he believes to be the essence of modern art, is not confined to the moment when the artist stands before the canvas or when the writer takes up his pen. Tzara insists that it is a way of life influencing every form of expression in an individual. Never losing sight of certain political and social concepts, Tzara asserts that the work of art must strike a common chord in humanity. It cannot be an isolated personal statement but must instead be the expression of collective and "non-directed" thought.

> Que ce soient les formes, les couleurs, les volumes, les sons ou les mots qui entrent comme médiateurs dans la réalisation de la chose signifiée, c'est en niant leur nature spécifique que l'artiste les rend aptes à agir dans un monde où ils seront réintégrés suivant la nouvelle nature plus générale qui désormais leur est attachée.[46]

> [Whether it be forms, colors, volumes, sounds, or words which enter as mediators in the working out of the thing

communicated, it is by denying their specific nature that the artist renders them capable of acting in a world where they will be reintegrated according to the new and more general nature which henceforth is attached to them.]

One of the facets of Picasso's work which seems to interest Tzara particularly is the constant evolution of his work, the fact that he has never settled on one particular style. Tzara, believer in dialectical materialism, is delighted by the *fougue* of Picasso's artistic evolution.

L'évolution de la peinture de Picasso est d'ordre cyclique, elle procède par bonds et ruptures et le heurt antagoniste des courants explorés, chacun inhibé par le suivant, à un degré supérieur nié et assimilé, provoque ces fulgurantes surprises de l'esprit qui ont contribué à assainir l'atmosphère viciée de la complaisance artistique.[47]

[The evolution of Picasso's painting is of a cyclical order. It proceeds by bounds, interruptions, and the antagonistic shock of the currents explored. Each of these is denied, negated, and assimilated by the following, provoking the brilliant mental surprises which have helped to clear the air which had been poisoned by artistic complaisance.]

This evolution, by the way, is not without reference to Tzara's own poetic evolution, for although Tzara retains certain basic ideas throughout his career, there is a great deal of difference between his first published collection of poetry, *Vingt-Cinq Poèmes*,[48] and the poems published after World War II.[49] Tzara's political beliefs predispose him to value constant change in an artist's production as a reflection of the broader change in social and economic structure. Tzara says that Picasso, through his artistic searching, reflects this change in reverse.

> On dirait que Picasso a refait le chemin au cours duquel furent inventées les formes plastiques depuis les arts anonymes jusqu'aux expressions savantes des temps modernes. En reconsidérant les moyens d'expression par lesquels l'homme s'est efforcé au long des âges de synthétiser sa représentation du monde, Picasso a nié non seulement l'objet de cette représentation, mais aussi les schèmes d'interprétation cristallisés à des époques et sous des latitudes différentes.[50]

> [You might say that Picasso has retraced the path along which plastic forms, from the anonymous arts to the skillful expressions of modern times, have been invented. By reexamining the means of expression by which man has forced himself through the ages to synthesize his representation of the world, Picasso has denied not only the object of that representation but also the schemes of interpretation which had hardened at different periods and in different parts of the world.]

It is true of Tzara as well as of Picasso that the traditional forms of representation, consecrated by the past, are denied. Tzara, like Picasso, is an enemy of the "cristallisé."

Tzara remarks that each of Picasso's works is the start of a new cycle; indeed in each canvas Picasso, searching to enlarge man's comprehension of nature through his visual and tactile senses, reinvents painting.[51]

This pursuit is not unlike the scientific search for knowledge; indeed the key to Tzara's vision of art through dada, surrealism, and postsurrealism may perhaps be found in this effort to change art from an aesthetic to a scientific pursuit. In speaking of Picasso, Tzara expresses the idea that the work of art is an experiment, an invention. This is certainly an understandable position taken by the inventor of "le rêve expérimental." The work of art is an attempt to pry loose a hidden truth, and it must be kept in mind that the work itself is of less importance than the search or the mental state that gave rise to it.

Tzara's insistence on his aversion to the enslavement of "finitude" in a work is particularly significant. He contends that classicism with its "closed systems" must give way to a new and less presumptuous aesthetic. He praises Picasso for not abiding by traditional concepts of perfection and completion in a work. In doing this, he very astutely describes an important element in modern art. It has been said of Jackson Pollock, for example, that his paintings have no focal point and could be "continued indefinitely without loss of character."[52]

Tzara believes that this is an age of tentativeness rather than one of grandiose metaphysical theories, and that art cannot fail to be influenced by this orientation. Tzara's article on Picasso is a kind of postsurrealist *Proclamation sans Prétention*, presenting theories which have led to such innovations in art as the "action painting" of Philip Guston and the graph music of Morton Feldman. In each of these cases the emphasis is often on the creative act rather than on the product of this act.

Tzara began his career when certain basic ideas were found wanting. He was a young man when commonly accepted scientific means of attaining knowledge were found to be inadequate. He was deeply influenced by these ideas which showed the ever-changing, elusive nature of man and the physical world. His answer is a new, approximate, and experimental manner in art, one which he asserts has been practiced by his friend Pablo Picasso. The constant experiments of Picasso are fruitful, according to Tzara, because they restore to man the plenitude that society has taken from him and, through love, give promise of a triumphant future.

Turning from Picasso, let us now examine Tzara's remarks about Rimbaud.[53] Rimbaud naturally appeals to Tzara not only for his poetry but also for the political ideas which he expressed.[54] In fact, Rimbaud speaks for Tzara when he says:

> When shall we go beyond shores and mountains, to greet the birth of new labors, the new wisdom, the putting to flight of tyrants and demons, the end of superstition, and worship—the very first!—Noel on earth.[55]

Tzara asserts that, for Rimbaud, 1873 marked not only the violent and tragic break with Verlaine, but also his discovery of the uselessness of literature. When *Une Saison en Enfer* was finished during the summer of 1873, Rimbaud made an important decision which was later to have a considerable influence on the dadaists and surrealists.[56] Rimbaud finally became certain that all art was folly and all intellectual speculation futile. He was convinced, according to Tzara ". . . de la vanité de toute tentative métaphysique de résoudre les antinomies de la vie." [57] [. . . of the futility of any metaphysical attempt to resolve life's contradictions.] Tzara calls *Une Saison en Enfer* ". . . un déchaînement primordial où étaient rassemblés tous les élans libérateurs en quête d'un absolu moral." [58] "C'est une pure énergie . . . éternellement en quête de spectacles insensés." [59] [. . . a primordial outburst in which all the liberating impulses were assembled in search of a moral absolute. It is pure energy . . . eternally in quest of mad scenes.] This search for a moral absolute and for "spectacles insensés" certainly would bring the dadaists close to Rimbaud.

For Tzara, *Une Saison en Enfer* is the last testament of Rimbaud the solitary rebel. Tzara asserts that the Rimbaud who had previously scorned other people suddenly became aware of their existence, and that, consequently, *Une Saison en Enfer,* which was a selfish and futureless experience, gave way to a more responsible and "outer-directed" orientation.

Tzara claims that to speak of the failure of Rimbaud is to confuse his real aim. For Tzara, Rimbaud's repudiation of poetry and the eventual silence of Harrar do not constitute a defeat but rather should be thought of as a movement to another plane, one that may be identified with "poésie-activité de l'esprit." Rimbaud had no concern for what he left behind. He was not in the least interested in furnishing posterity with an artistic legacy. For him, the movement toward knowledge and ultimate self-realization was all-important.

> Pour Rimbaud lui-même, il ne s'agissait que d'exprimer sa personnalité à travers la substance d'une vie absorbante, multiple et indivisible, . . . sans nullement se soucier de ce que, dans sa course précipitée, il abandonnait derrière lui.[60]

> [For Rimbaud himself it was only a matter of expressing his personality through the means of an absorbing, multiple, and indivisible life . . . without in any way caring about what, in his precipitous dash, he left behind.]

This minimization of the work itself is one of the keys to Tzara's theories on art. His emphasis is on the mind behind the work, and he finds Rimbaud's mental attitude particularly rich in significance. Rimbaud's abandonment of poetry is rather a reduction of poetry to more human terms. It is no longer a formal pursuit, no longer "un métier," but a manner of confronting the world. Thus the meaning of the title, "L'Unité de Rimbaud," becomes apparent. In Tzara's opinion, Rimbaud's life is not divided into creation and abdication; it is a unified whole, the second part of his life—from 1873 on—being the logical and necessary outcome of the first—all of it unified in a drive toward what Tzara calls "poésie-état d'esprit."

Tzara insists that Rimbaud's life in Africa is not explained by speaking of abject surrender to bourgeois values. Rimbaud's African role was that of a pioneer, and a heroic one at that. Claiming that Rimbaud's existence at Harrar must be understood in the perspective of a particular historical moment, Tzara asserts that Rimbaud may have thought himself a "peaceful conqueror," one who would bring culture to black Africa.

Il est le précurseur, le conquérant pacifique, le brasseur d'hommes et de matières premières pour qui l'échange entre l'Orient et L'Occident est un facteur de progrès. Sa vision poétique d'ingénieur cherche un débouché de grande envergure, le terrain pratique pour se réaliser. Il est le prophète et l'instrument de ce monde scientifique dont l'avenir se résout en une féerie de confort, de plénitude, de vitesse et d'entente entre les peuples et les races différentes.[61]

[He is the precursor, the peaceful conqueror, the big dealer in men and raw materials for whom trade between the Orient and the Occident is an agent of progress. His poetic vision as an engineer searches for a large-scale market and the practical terrain for its accomplishment. He is the prophet and instrument of this scientific world whose future is changed into a Utopia of comfort, plenty, speed, and of understanding between different peoples and races.]

Tzara attempts to justify Rimbaud's actions in Africa by saying that what we would today consider reprehensible was heroic in the nineteenth century. The critic may ask what proof Tzara can offer in support of his view of Rimbaud, and in particular of the interpretation of Rimbaud's role in Africa. The edition prefaced by Tzara's remarks includes an important selection of Rimbaud's letters. One might expect that what Tzara called a heroic vision, if there were one, would be expressed in the correspondence, but Tzara is forced to admit that the letters do not substantiate his theory. He claims that they do not simply because the people to whom they were written—Rimbaud's mother, for example—would have been unable to understand the meaning of such a vision. This effort to create a crusading engineer out of Rimbaud is most unconvincing.

It is interesting, however, to note that Tzara places so much emphasis on Rimbaud's life and so little on his work. This causes him to be particularly censorious of critics who focus on Rimbaud's poetry. Tzara is especially reproachful of the thesis advanced by Jacques Gengoux which would explain Rimbaud's work as a mechanical trick involving the displacement of vowels.[62] "Que devient dans cette mécanique montée de toutes pièces son impulsivité explosive qui, aussi bien dans ses écrits que dans sa vie, gonfle cet être de soleil?" [63] [What becomes, in that completely trumped-up construction, of his explosive impulsiveness which, as much in his writings as in his life, swelled Rimbaud with the sun's light?] One would imagine that for Tzara the critic must above all be a biographer if not a psychologist, and that his task is to understand "l'approfondissement d'un processus continu et non pas volonté réfléchie d'obéir à des règles extérieures à *cette action vécue* [my italics] qu'est toute poésie." [64] [the analysis of a continual process and not the thought-out decision to obey rules outside of *that experienced action* which all poetry is.] Tzara warns that one must not confuse real poetic tension with the cleverness of versifiers.

Tzara makes an interesting point in asserting that Rimbaud is also significant for his rejection of the passive sentimentality in many romantic poets. Rimbaud refused to bend under the immense weight of the romantic force of nature. He did not accept its law because such acceptance is fraught with great danger. Tzara, fighter against fascism, could testify that any such mystique is often a justification for inhumanity. Throughout his entire life, Tzara opposed

. . . ceux enfin, qui prétendent contenir une parcelle de ce sublime naturel qui, soit d'essence sacrée, soit simplement élevée au niveau de cette force par un acte magique de participation ou d'initiation est destiné à maintenir dans une

terreur permanente la masse des hommes que l'on voudrait
voir éternellement consentants.[65]

[. . . those who claim to possess a part of that natural sub-
limity which, either of a sacred essence or simply elevated to
that status by a magical act of participation or initiation, is
intended to maintain the masses, whom some would like to
see eternally consenting, in a state of permanent terror.]

Rimbaud's solution to an imperfect world was revolt, not
resignation and consent. Instead of accepting a blind and
stupid fatalism, he showed that man must fight to liberate
himself from the constraints of his present condition. His
example is one of continual "dépassement," which finally
ends by going beyond art itself.

L'exemple de Rimbaud nous atteint toujours en plein
centre de notre sensibilité. Sa virulence s'exprime par un
constant dépassement: dépassement des valeurs esthétiques
qu'il a créées, dépassement des limites de son temps.[66]

[Rimbaud's example touches us in the very center of our
feelings. His virulence expresses itself by a constant overstepping—overstepping of esthetic values which he created,
and overstepping the limits of his age.]

Tzara's criticism is primarily an attempt to explain and
justify Rimbaud's decision to give up poetry to become a
businessman. This interpretation of heroic "dépassement"
is unacceptable. One should look to Albert Camus for a

simpler and more convincing explanation of Harrar.[67] Camus asserts that Rimbaud's development is no more puzzling than "the mystery attached to the banality achieved by brilliant young girls whom marriage transforms into adding or sewing machines."[68] Camus seems to be right in saying that it often takes more courage to live with one's genius than to deny it. He also is more frank than Tzara when he speaks of the letters in which Rimbaud reveals himself to be avaricious and more worried about his seventeen pound money belt giving him dysentery than about bringing civilization to Africa. Although Camus appreciates Rimbaud's poetry fully as much as Tzara, he does not hesitate to assert that Rimbaud succumbed to the temptation of nihilism and found his at Harrar.

Tzara's comments on Rimbaud, Henri Rousseau, Corbière, and Picasso reveal certain central concepts that give coherence to his entire critical outlook. One of these basic concepts is that poetry must be lived, that it cannot merely be the fruit of study or imagination but must be anchored in experience. Related to this view is Tzara's strongly anti-romantic sentiment expressed in his criticism, for he opposes mysticism with *le quotidien* and rhetoric with conversation. For flights of eloquence, Tzara would substitute the expression of man's daily experience and his struggle to forge a better world. The poet can contribute to this goal, for his poetry is in itself a means of attaining knowledge.

These recurring general principles are evident in Tzara's

shorter articles on such other literary figures as Pierre Reverdy,[69] Paul Eluard,[70] Guillaume Apollinaire,[71] and René Crevel.[72] They also furnish the answer to why Tzara has shown interest in Villon.[73] On the surface this interest in Villon appears surprising, since Tzara's main concern, as we have seen, has been with certain writers and painters from the "Bousingots" to the surrealists. What does Villon have in common with a poet like Apollinaire? The answer lies in Tzara's extreme anti-romantic position. He sees in both Villon and Apollinaire the expression of opposition to the poetry that preceded them, a poetry less solidly immersed than theirs in everyday existence. In Apollinaire, Tzara finds the continuation of an anti-rhetorical tradition which was upheld by Villon, Rimbaud, and Verlaine. Tzara extolls a simplicity and directness of expression in these poets; in fact, he explains Apollinaire's neglect of punctuation by saying that strict adherence to grammatical rules would have hampered the immediacy and power of Apollinaire's poems. Tzara surely realized that Villon's poetry was written with rigid formal structures in mind, but he suggests that Villon's will to communicate was stronger than his preoccupation with structure. Tzara particularly appreciates Villon's attention to everyday matters. He sees Villon's primary significance in his opposition to the sentimentality of such precursors as Charles d'Orléans. Instead of presenting an idealized concept of love and nature, Villon treats the brute facts of his everyday existence, using a simple and direct style. Tzara interprets Baudelaire's significance in much the same manner:

> En actualisant la réalité de la vie quotidienne, sous toutes ses faces, physiques et morales, il a introduit dans la vie des idées une clairvoyance qui a fini par chasser les chimères romantiques dont s'encombrait la jeunesse d'alors, avide d'avancer.[74]

> [By objectifying the reality of everyday life in all its physical and moral facets, he introduced into the life of ideas a clairvoyance which ended up by chasing away the romantic chimeras saddling the youth of that time, eager to move ahead.]

The recurring words in Tzara's criticism of these poets are: "langage oral," "la vie quotidienne," and "réalité vécue." They are also the qualities that Tzara finds and admires in Paul Eluard's poetry. "Le propre d'Eluard est d'avoir réussi à incorporer à sa poésie les attributs capables de la faire passer dans le langage commun." [75] [The characteristic of Eluard is to have succeeded in incorporating into his poetry the attributes that could make it pass into common speech.] This tendency to write poetry which is very close to everyday speech (a tendency totally absent from the mystifications and anti-communicative nature of dada) has its roots in political belief. "Car cette tendance elle-même découle de son aspiration idéologique ayant en vue la construction d'un monde fondé sur la communion de tous et la liberté." [76] [Because that tendency itself comes from his ideological aspiration which looks for the construction of a world founded on freedom and the communion of all.]

Tzara calls for poetic images to be well defined. He says that Eluard's images are good in that they are supremely concrete and have nothing discursive about them. Images must be concrete and they must be rooted in personal experience. Paying tribute to Pierre Reverdy, Tzara says:

> Pierre Reverdy semble être le poète qui a le mieux saisi le sens de ce que doit être l'image vécue; sa poésie, dont les racines sont plantées dans le sol du quotidien s'élève, par-dessus la logique habituelle, à une intelligence approfondie du monde environnant.[77]

> [Pierre Reverdy seems to be the poet who best grasped the meaning of what the lived image should be. His poetry, whose roots are planted in the soil of the commonplace, raises itself beyond customary logic to a profound understanding of the surrounding world.]

Finally, René Crevel is mentioned as another example of a poet who realized that there must be no separation between life and poetry. Tzara asserts that Crevel was one of the purest representatives of a generation of poets for whom life and poetry were one.[78]

Thus, for Tzara, a poet must be completely caught up in the current of history. His life and work must be a unified whole, and his role must be that of a seeker for knowledge, directly and simply communicating his discoveries to his fellow men. Much of French poetry from the *Trobar Clus* through Maurice Scève and Mallarmé has been a scholarly and hermetic poetry. Rejecting this tradition and renouncing the mystification and secret society that was dada, Tzara progressively moves toward a critical position which adopts directness, simplicity, and the expression of the everyday as guiding principles. Jean Cassou has called Tzara's poetic evolution one toward "la poésie humaniste." It seems proper to apply the same term to Tzara as a critic, recognizing his position as one of France's most persuasive "critiques humanistes."

7   *Le Surréalisme et l'Après-Guerre*

In assessing the general critical vision of Tristan Tzara, one should concentrate on three main considerations: his interpretation of dadaism, his criticism of surrealism, and, finally, his theory of poetry. It is appropriate to refer to Tzara's *Le Surréalisme et l'Après-Guerre* [1] for this conclusion, since this book presents theories which had been put to test by the war and which he had judged to be well founded. *Le Surréalisme et l'Après-Guerre* is not only Tzara's major critical work, but it retains its validity because in no subsequent article did he modify positions set forth in this book.

Le Surréalisme et l'Après-Guerre is the text of a speech given by Tzara at the Sorbonne on the eleventh of April, 1947, and of another speech given in December 1946, and February 1947, at the French Institutes of Bucharest

Figure 20. Tzara at the Sorbonne, April 11, 1947. Tzara is at the desk at left; André Breton stands at middle right shouting and pointing a finger. Reproduced from Georges Ribemont-Dessaignes, *Déja Jadis*, p. 177 (Paris: René Julliard, 1958).

and Prague. The Sorbonne speech was the occasion of a demonstration against Tzara which was led by a group of surrealists. A photograph in Ribemont-Dessaigne's *Déjà Jadis* shows Breton on his feet, shaking his fist at his former friend, who is seated on the podium. The scene is strongly reminiscent of the *Cœur à Gaz* incident; the surroundings alone seem an odd battleground for Tzara and Breton—a theatre would be more appropriate than an amphitheatre at the University of Paris. This book, the culmination of Tzara's critical thought, offers both a backward look at the broad evolution of modern poetry with special emphasis on dada and surrealism, and a forward look at the poetry of the future and its relationship to revolution.

The remarks Tzara made in 1947 concerning dada were obviously colored by his political beliefs. His retrospective view of dada seems to err in two respects. Dada was something more than he claimed, and it was something less. Tzara asserted that dada was born out of a moral requirement, the need that he felt (with his friends) to be uncompromising in a search for absolute truth untainted by preconceived historical, moral, or aesthetic ideas.[2] Tzara contended that the dadaists wanted to place man above the abstract concepts which had impoverished his existence. The dadaist showed his disgust with a corrupt culture by saying no and by living spontaneously and creatively so that his life itself became his artistic creation. He wrote only with the intention of sabotaging *belles-*

lettres and attacking logic through language. This appraisal of dada is fair, but it is also very limited. Dada has far greater significance than Tzara admits, for it is a symptom of a nineteenth- and twentieth-century *crise de conscience*. Dada is a consequence of a gradual dissolution of values in the Western World which reached a point of crisis in the second decade of this century. Religion, allied with national states, continued to be less and less of a directing force for many intellectuals, certain aspects of science were under attack, and there was compelling evidence that patriotism was being severely undermined.[3] This in part was the climate that gave birth to dada.

Dada was, as Tzara contends, an attempt by a small group of artists to expose language through nonsensical fulminations and stammerings and to humble what the dadaists thought to be over-pretentious and mendacious in their culture. However, the fact that, from the beginning, this movement drew its adherents from widely scattered parts of the world, and that even today, over a half century later, a growing number of young artists choose to call themselves neo-dadaists, demonstrates that the general attitude of dada is of real significance in our modern world. Dada is thus something more than Tzara was willing to concede in 1947. It was also something less.

The dada movement in Switzerland and France was less politically oriented than Tzara would have us believe. Orthodox Marxists criticize dada because of its extreme nihilism. To offset this criticism, Tzara claims that the Zurich dadaists were not only aware of the Russian Revolution but were in fact in sympathy with it. Tzara asserts that this revolution was seen by his fellow avant-gardists in Zurich as a glimmer of hope for mankind. Such a statement is hard to refute, but there is no documentary proof to bear it out. Though German dadaism was political from the beginning, there is no real evidence that the Zurich dadaists were even aware of the significance of Lenin who was living practically in their midst. Marcel Janco merely says of the Cabaret Voltaire: "Out of the thick smoke, in the middle of the noise of declamations or of a popular song, there were sudden apparitions, like Lenin, surrounded by a group." [4] Hugo Ball, making no mention of politics, says in his diary: "What strange happenings! At the time when our cabaret was located at number 1 Spiegelgasse in Zurich, across from us, living at number 6 of the same street, was a man whose name, if I'm not mistaken, was Ulianow-Lenin." [5] It has been said that Lenin and Tzara played chess together in the Cabaret Voltaire, but that may be apocryphal. Whether he knew Lenin or not, Tzara does claim to have sympathized with the Russian Revolution, saying that when Fritz Platten returned to Zurich from Russia in 1917 with precise details of the revolution which the press had systematically concealed, a riot broke out, followed by a general strike. Tzara claims that it was his wish that the general strike might spread to the belligerent countries, thus putting an end to the war.[6] It must be said that this wish is not expressed in any of the dada publications.

Tzara also claims that he welcomed the revolution even more enthusiastically as an antidote to the sniveling pacifism that sapped the moral fiber of those who would later carry on the social struggle.[7] He claims that Hugo Ball and Walter Serner agreed with him on this point. If this is true, it means that Hugo Ball must have changed radically from 1916, at which time he wrote in *Flight from Time*: "Since no art, *politics* [my italics] or religious faith seems adequate to dam this torrent, there remains only the blague and the bleeding pose." [8] Tzara attempts to justify this "bleeding pose," which was a substitute for direct political action on dada's part, by saying that the time was not ripe in France after the war for a direct social struggle. The middle class had consolidated its position through victory, and its strength prevented dada from being anything other than negative and individualistic.[9] However, "il est certain que *la table rase* dont nous faisions le principe directeur de notre activité, n'avait de valeur que dans la mesure où *autre chose* devait lui succéder." [10] [it is certain that the *blank slate* which we had made the guiding principle of our actions only had value to the extent to which *something else* would follow it.] The "autre chose" was of course surrealism, to which Tzara would give allegiance as long as it was involved in the social conflict.

In Tzara's opinion surrealism had failed in many respects. It had failed notably in its inability to wed dream to action. Its lack of rigorous ideology and its silence during the Second World War are also cited as major shortcomings. Tzara insists that, to have validity, poetry must be lived. It must be the result of a profound moral commitment which will not allow the poet to indulge himself in any purely aesthetic pursuit. These, in general, are accusations which Tzara levels at surrealism. His career as a surrealist and his views in retrospect on this movement illustrate a fundamental dichotomy which has plagued surrealism almost from its inception. There have been two surrealist camps: those who are interested in art mainly as an adjunct to revolutionary politics, and those who view surrealism primarily as an attack on aesthetic conventions. Despite repeated efforts by Breton to bridge the gap, it continued, until the politically minded completely disavowed surrealism. This, of course, was the case with Tzara.

He does, however, praise the original goal of surrealism, which he describes as the eventual liberation of man and the reconciliation of dream and action. At the same time, he laments the fact that the surrealists produced more in the realm of dream than of action. The fusion of dream and conscious action, in Tzara's opinion, could only be brought about through certain definite political steps. One attempt at such a reconciliation did occur in the early thirties with Vaillant-Couturier's founding of the Association des Ecrivains et Artistes Révolutionnaires. This, according to Tzara, was a worthwhile attempt, but he expresses serious reservations about the surrealists' acceptance and interpretation of Marxism. Other efforts at reconciling dream and action were Aragon's trip to Kharkov in 1931 and the 1933 founding of La Maison de la Culture, to which Tzara and his friend René Crevel adhered. Tzara asserts that the increased tempo of fascist activity necessitated increased political *engagement* on the part of the writer. The weight of ominous events required that he immerse himself in a practical opposition to fascism, which was jeopardizing social justice all over Europe. Literature and politics became necessarily connected; poetry was plunged "up to its neck in history." [11] But, though Tzara speaks out for "engaged" poetry, a short excerpt from one of his Spanish Civil War poems shows that in his own work, poetic quality is not abandoned in favor of a message.

Espagne 1936

jeunesse des pas dans la cendre
le soleil dévoile ta matinale surdité
lorsque le serpent se mêle de labourer
aux lentes fonderies de cristal
les crêtes tannées de peau et de lait

sous la force mâle des oiseaux
a percé le cri en armes de l'hiver
pleurez femmes si le cœur vous en dit
les matelots protègeront vos larmes. [12]

[Spain 1936

youth of steps in the ashes
the sun unveils your morning deafness
when the serpent takes a hand in plowing
by the slow foundries of crystal
the tanned crests of skin and of milk

under the male force of the birds
the shout pierced the winter's arms
cry, women, if your heart tells you to
the sailors will protect your tears.]

The profusion of images in Tzara's poetry makes any single "message" hard to pick out; nevertheless his constant assertion is that art is not an end in itself but should be subordinated to a higher end: the liberation of man. Man had to be freed of his material shackles and his moral restraints.[13] While surrealism could conceivably carry out the latter task, communism was seen as the only possible way to liberate man economically.

Tzara strongly criticized surrealism for being absent during the war. He believed that there was no historical justification for a movement which was of absolutely no help in the occupation. André Breton spent the war years outside of France, and Tzara points out that the only surrealist review to appear during the war, *VVV*, was of a very "arty" and expensive nature. This objection is the same one which, in part, decided him to sever all connection with *Minotaure* in the thirties. Tzara is justly

bitter over some of the "jeux surréalistes" described in
VVV. One of them had to do with placing a hand on
either side of a wire fence and running the hands up and
down touching each other. Tzara simply and devastat-
ingly remarks that this was probably the only surrealist
experience at the time that had anything to do with the
occupation, where, "dans les camps de concentration . . .
les prisonniers . . . en fait de grillages étaient devenus de
véritables spécialistes." [14] ["prisoners in the concentration
camps had become veritable specialists in the matter of
wire fencing."] Tzara's bitterness with respect to surrealism very likely comes from the unreasonably high
hopes he once held for the movement. To one who has not
been a surrealist, it is less surprising that this interesting
and productive literary and artistic group could not com-
bat the horrors of war and occupation.

Another criticism leveled at surrealism by Tzara is with
respect to its preoccupation with love. Tzara asserts that
the surrealists attempted to reconcile Freud and Marx, and
that they failed in the process. Tzara has pointed out that
love is simply part of a superstructure dependent on the
basic economic structure, and that consequently it is of
somewhat less interest than the surrealists had thought.[15]
His argument is weak, if not absurd. One of the glories of
surrealism has been its exaltation of love in such works
as Breton's *Nadja,* or Max Ernst's sequence, "Desire," in
the film, *Dreams That Money Can Buy.* Above all, who
has sung more beautifully of love than the man who wrote
the following lines:

Elle est debout sur mes paupières
Et ses cheveux sont dans les miens,
Elle a la forme de mes mains,
Elle a la couleur de mes yeux,
Elle s'engloutit dans mon ombre
Comme une pierre sur le ciel.

Elle a toujours les yeux ouverts
Et ne me laisse pas dormir.
Ses rêves en pleine lumière
Font s'évaporer les soleils,
Me font rire, pleurer et rire,
Parler sans avoir rien à dire.[16]

[She stands on my eyelids and her hair is in mine. She has the shape of my hands, she has the color of my eyes, she is swallowed up in my shadow like a stone on the sky.

Her eyes are always open and she doesn't let me sleep. Her dreams in broad daylight make suns evaporate, make me laugh, cry and laugh, speak without having anything to say.]

Unacceptable too is Tzara's accusation that the surrealists have always expressed a pessimistic view of man's possibilities.[17] Tzara affirms that surrealism was a movement of despair and that its poetry was usually negative. This is certainly not the case. Optimism is a trait which was more or less present in most surrealist poetry, in sharp contrast to that of the symbolists. The surrealist movement was founded on the belief that man had immense capabilities which could be opened up, and that, although society was not what it should be, it could be changed. Tzara only differs in his conviction that new poetry must be socialist inspired.[18] However, when an artist's work is in the service of a political dream, it quite often loses its artistic value completely. A striking case in point is post-surrealist poetry, such as Louis Aragon's *Les Yeux et la Mémoire,* or Paul Eluard's *Les Sentiers et les Routes de la Poésie.*[19] Tzara should know that "experimental" dreams are always better than well-rehearsed ones.

For Tzara, surrealism is a product of a moribund civilization, a last aesthetic rattle before the end. Forms of society are mortal, but man, he believed, endures, and the poet's duty is to be "au service de ses besoins, de ses désirs, tel qu'il est et qu'en lui-même il se change."[20] [in the service of his needs and desires, such as he is and such as to himself he transforms himself.] Tzara paraphrases Mallarmé (with a significant change) with a view to expressing his conviction that if man is today only approximate, he is on his way to full realization of his potentialities. It is noteworthy that Tzara seems to be saying that poetry is at its best when it is in the service of the individual. And being in the service of the individual is for Tzara the same thing as being in the service of the revolution or of humanity. At any rate, the implication is clear that the only positive and optimistic poetry, the poetry of the future, will have to come from a poet deeply involved in political struggle. It is Tzara's contention that not only can there be such a thing as "engaged" poetry, but that in fact "engagement" is the only valid justification for being a poet.

What is striking about this concept is the refusal to abandon imagination in favor of socialist realism. His will to proclaim the rights of imagination parallels that of the eminent philosopher, Gaston Bachelard.[21] Bachelard, however, is free of the political considerations which weaken Tzara's argument. Tzara's thesis from the mid-thirties was that true poetry, or oneiric experience, is suppressed by our capitalistic society. He also asserts that the most significant French poetry from the eighteenth century to today has expressed an attempt to liberate itself from logic and threadbare linguistic conventions in order to return to its source which is dream. This, of course, would make poetry a common heritage that could radiate over all of life's phenomena. Tzara calls for poetry to express common dynamic collective images, recognizing that: "un certain animisme continue à subsister sous forme de représentation métaphorique." [22] [a certain animism continues to exist in the form of metaphoric representations.] In his opinion, the essence of poetry is in the recapture and expression of these myths which our rationally ordered society has subverted.

Tzara asserts that poetry narrows the gap between dream and wakefulness and thus has a healthy function. It assumes a necessary and utilitarian role instead of merely providing complacent sensual enjoyment.[23] This is a very important point; it should be remembered that Tzara criticized poetry as *jouissance* from the time of the *Seven Dada Manifestoes*. He is supported on this point by both Gaston Bachelard and the psychologist Otto Rank. Bachelard claims that it is as serious to be deprived of the irrational as it is to be deprived of a grasp of reality. Indeed, according to Bachelard, one who does not practice what Tzara calls poetry is very likely a neurotic.[24] Otto Rank also affirms that one must accept and even *live* the irrational, rediscovering human values "beyond psychology."[25] Tzara continued to contend that these values were intact in primitive societies and that poetry was considered an integral part of everyday life. His wish is to elevate poetry to the importance it once had in these less civilized cultures. He calls for poetry to become once again, if not religious, at least magical and communal. When he praises the old epics like *Gilgamesh* and some of the poems in the Bible which "répondaient à des nécessités précises que l'histoire et le mythe confondus exigeaient d'une manière impérieuse . . . et exaltaient les sentiments religieux et nationaux et exprimaient les volontés populaires dans leur marche vers le progrès,"[26] [answered precise needs which history and myth together imperiously demanded . . . and exalted religious and national sentiments, expressing the popular wishes in their march toward progress,] he is explicitly showing that his aesthetic is a strong reaction against art for art's sake. He decries the shift from these epics, which expressed collective sentiments, to a more personal poetry. Although his views on poetry often owe a great deal to psychology, Tzara does not lose sight of the dependence of these ideas on Marxist doctrine. For him, all poetry, whether the expression of "directed" or "non-directed" thought, is always dependent upon prevailing economic and social structures, as is the place of the poet in society. The poet in a capitalistic society is always a rebel, having as his task the crushing of "la dureté conceptuelle du langage en ce que celui-ci, dans l'emploi qu'en fait le poète, contient encore soit de trop utilitaire, soit de mécaniquement logique ou de nettement descriptif." [27] [the conceptual rigidity of language to the extent to which that language, as the poet uses it, still contains either too much of the utilitarian or too much of the mechanically logical or plainly descriptive.] We shall see some implications of this attack on language in the final chapter.

8 Lettrism

Rimbaud's silence, Tristan Corbière's "verbal exaspera-tion," and Tzara's preoccupation with the problem of language and its inadequacy are all manifestations of a modern crisis of the word. Perhaps Tzara's greatest signi-ficance lies in the important part he plays in elucidating this problem through his critical writings. He is not only prominent in illustrating a modern breakdown in com-munication, but is in fact a champion of this verbal crisis. Critical consideration of one outgrowth of this dadaist and surrealist attack on language, lettrism, provides a key for understanding the import of this preoccupation.

Lettrism is an offspring of dada. This would make Tzara its grandfather, and indeed two prominent lettrists, Mau-rice Lemaître and Isidore Isou, were present at Tzara's burial in the Montparnasse cemetery, Lemaître with the intention of reading a lettrist "Epître à Tristan Tzara" despite "the opposition by Tzara's family and the insults, menaces and provocations of the Stalinists. . . ." [1]

Figure 21. Maurice Lemaître and Isidore Isou at Tzara's burial in Montparnasse Cemetery, Paris. Photo courtesy Maurice Lemaître.

The lettrists, who have replaced the Biblical "In the beginning was the word," with "In the beginning was the croak," appear to be the new dadaists. Richard Huelsenbeck, ex-dadaist and one of the most lucid interpreters of this movement, has asserted that the principles of "bruitism," simultaneity, and collage underlie the entire production of dada. It is the affirmation of one of these principles, "bruitism," and its elevation to the status of a dogma, which have given rise to lettrism. Huelsenbeck, in his history of dada, says that "bruitism is a kind of return to nature. It is the music produced by circuits of atoms; death ceases to be an escape of the soul from earthly misery and becomes a vomiting, screaming and choking." [2] The *bruitist* concerts given by the dadaists at the Cabaret Voltaire consisted of a clanging of pots and pans, whistles, shouts, and banging on any convenient object. Lettrism reduces this cacophony to one produced solely by the human voice; "bruitage" becomes purely verbal.

Hugo Ball describes the details of one of his Cabaret Voltaire performances of a "sound poem."

My legs were covered with a cothurnus of luminous blue cardboard, which reached up to my hips so that I looked like an obelisk. Above that I wore a huge cardboard collar that was scarlet inside and gold outside. This was fastened at the throat in such a manner that I was able to move it like wings by raising and dropping my elbows. In addition I wore a hightop hat striped with blue and white. [3]

Figure 22. Hugo Ball reciting a "sound poem" at the Cabaret Voltaire in Zurich, 1916. Reproduced from Georges Ribemont-Dessaignes, *Déja Jadis*, p. 80 (Paris: René Julliard, 1958).

One can only imagine the effect produced by this queer bird which flapped its wings grotesquely and recited the following "verse":

gadji beri bimbi
glandridi lauli lonni cadori
grandjama bim beri glassala
glandridi glassals tuffm i zimbrabim
blassa galassasa tuffm i zimbrabim . . .[4]

Ball was motivated by a belief that poetry must be something other than a form of conveying thought. He suggests that "we should withdraw into the innermost alchemy of the word, and even *surrender the word* [my italics], in this way conserving for poetry its most sacred domain." [5] One wonders what exactly this "sacred domain" of poetry is. Tzara's answer is: thought. Georges Hugnet, another dada scholar, remarks that Tzara expressed this most clearly in the "Essai sur la Situation de la Poésie," in quoting Lassailly and Borel

. . . who, by their use of *sound,* showed that they recognized the inadequacy of words as a vehicle for the logic of feelings, for the "ineffable, the inexpressible," as they put it, and for specifically poetical activity . . . Tzara cites still other instances to show that various poets . . . unconsciously sensed the existence of a spiritual activity exclusive of logic and the type of thought, which as Tzara wrote in one of the *7 manifestes dada* "is manufactured in the mouth." [6]

Figure 23. Sorbonne statue with graffito on its base, Paris, May 1968.
Reproduced from *L'Imagination au Pouvoir* (Paris: Eric Losfeld, 1968).

As a precursor of lettrism and an active practitioner of *bruitism*, Tzara wrote the following in "Pélamide," one of the *Vingt-Cinq Poèmes*:

a e ou o youyouyou i e ou o
youyouyou
drrdrrdrrgrrrgrrr [7]

Such a "poem" is perhaps to be expected from the director of the Société Anonyme pour l'Exploitation du Vocabulaire. This firm went into a temporary eclipse, however, and did not reappear until the end of World War II under the guise of lettrism. Isidore Isou, like Tzara of Rumanian origin, was the leader of this group.[8] Isou and lettrism were featured in a special issue of Max-Pol Fouchet's literary magazine, *Fontaine*, which was devoted to "Instances de la Poésie en 1947." [9]

A comparison between Isou and Tzara shows that Tzara's poetry has changed a great deal in certain respects. If Tzara's later poetic work is not always more intelligible than his early dada poems, at any rate, sound alone has been abandoned, and a certain *ampleur* in this poetry expresses a powerful inner lyricism. One cannot speak of lyricism in discussing Isou's movement which he describes in the following way: "La lettrie est l'art qui accepte la matière des lettres réduites et devenues simplement elles-mêmes (s'ajoutant ou remplaçant totalement les éléments poétiques et musicaux) et qui les dépasse pour mouler dans leur bloc des œuvres cohérentes." [10] [Lettrism is the art which accepts the substance of letters which are reduced and have become simply themselves (by adding or totally replacing the poetic and musical elements) and which goes beyond them in order to cast coherent works in one piece.]

Current literary criticism is particularly fascinated by French examples of "alittérature," "antiroman," and "antipièce." Isou, following the example of Tzara, presents what might be called an "antilinguistique." "Depuis l'existence du langage on a pressenti derrière lui un inconnu antilinguistique, abîme et boîte-à-ordures de nos moyens de transmission." [11] [Throughout the existence of language there has been a suspicion that behind language there was an antilinguistic unknown, a chasm and garbage can of our means of transmission.]

Like the surrealists and the dadaists, Isou takes pains to present his literary family tree and, surprisingly enough, claims Aristophanes and Molière as early lettrists. Aristophanes is quoted as having written:

Epopoi poi popoi, epopoi popoi, tiotiotiotiotiotiotio, trito, trioto, totbrix.[12]

Molière's "contribution" comes from *Le Bourgeois Gentilhomme:* "hou la ba ba; la chou, ba la, ba ba, la da, . . . Ambousahin oqui boraf." [13] Although this and other words such as "cacaracamouchen" are simply used to dupe Monsieur Jourdain, Isou interprets such gibberish as evidence

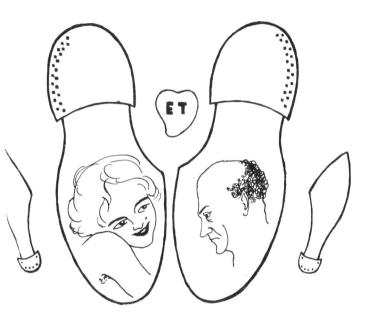

Figure 24. "Lits et Ratures," facsimile of the cover of *Littérature*, December 1, 1922. Photo courtesy Museum of Modern Art, N.Y.

that some great writers had dimly recognized the fact that poetry was something other than literature, a word which in avant-garde circles had been pejorative ever since its mocking use as the name of a journal, *Littérature*. The word was susceptible to different suggestions through its division into "Lits et Ratures" [Beds and Erasures], and "Lis tes Ratures" [Read your Erasures]. Despite this well-established anti-literary bias, Isou claims to have brought to light the suspicion that poetry has nothing to do with literature.[14] Rather than being simply a suspicion, this was one of the keystones of dada voiced repeatedly by Tzara. Any claim to originality in this domain by Isou would be extravagant. However, Isou and anti-literary henchmen such as the creative Lemaître did add another nineteen letters to the old alphabet, opening up, as he says, the old alphabet which had stagnated for centuries in its twenty-four arteriosclerosed letters and shoving into its belly nineteen new letters.[15] These new letters help create a musical effect which produces the euphoric state that the masses expect of art. Thus, sound poems have become a medium for bringing about "euphoric state." Poetry, which for Tzara has meant a search for knowledge, becomes a soporific. Its power to liberate is instead directed to comforting the masses, reassuring them by giving:

> . . . le plaisir de reconnaître, au delà du flou rythmique, un thème général, comme un cadre sous entendu, et flatte l'intelligence publique, en lui demandant l'effort minimum nécessaire pour saisir les allusions.[16]

[. . . the pleasure of recognizing beyond the rythmical softness a general theme, like an implied framework, and it flat-
ters the common intelligence by demanding of it the minimum effort necessary to grasp the allusions.]

In Chapter Five Tzara's language has been characterized
as a "language of indeterminacy," linking it with new
methods of investigation in the sciences typified by Heisenberg. Isou claims that Tzara's expression is even more up to
date, being the authentic voice of the atomic age.[17] Lettrist
poetry is made up of man's last croaks, gasps and gurgles
because:

Nous avons appris que les poèmes doivent siffler comme
les poumons des guerriers, que nos vers doivent s'écouler
aveugles comme leurs yeux, que nos lettres doivent éclater,
incompréhensibles, folles, et crépiter comme leurs cerveaux.[18]

[We have learned that poems must wheeze like the lungs
of warriors, that our verse must stream out, blinded like their
eyes, and that our letters must explode, incomprehensible,
mad, and sputter out like their brains.]

In Le Surréalisme et l'Après-Guerre, Tzara asserted that
history had bypassed surrealism. Isou is in complete agreement with Tzara on this point. Recognizing the fact that
dreams are a luxury in the age of the hydrogen bomb, Isou
says of surrealism: ". . . we talk to them about life and
they tell us their dreams."[19] He ridicules the mystical ef-

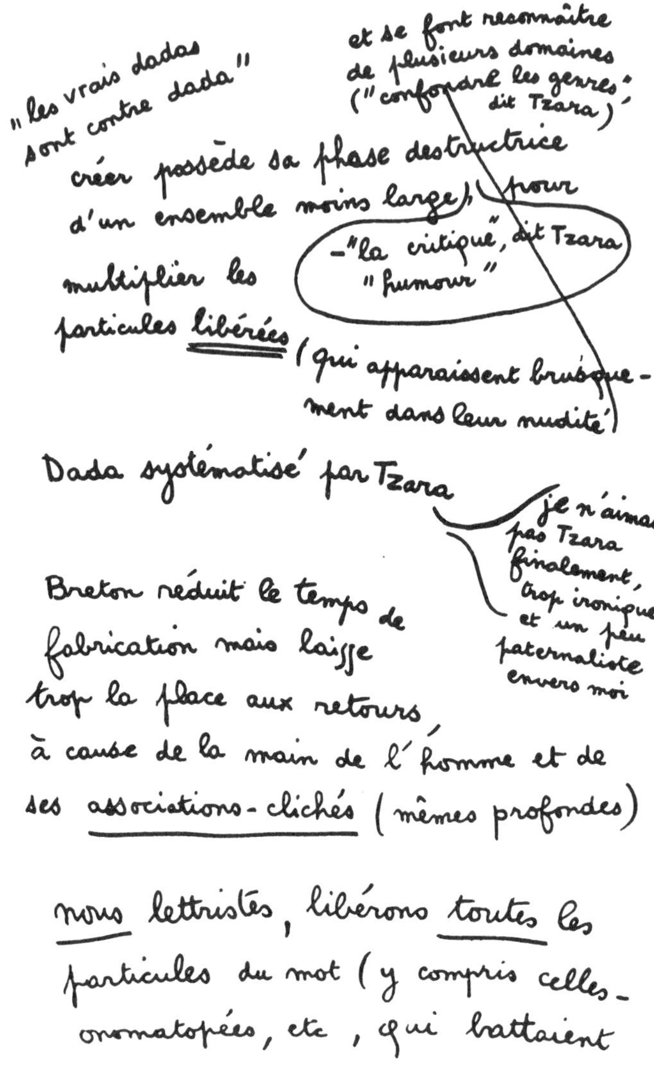

"les vrais dadas" / sont contre dada"

et se font reconnaître / de plusieurs domaines / ("confondre les genres", / dit Tzara)

créer possède sa phase destructrice / d'un ensemble moins large, / pour

multiplier les / particules libérées (qui apparaissent brusque- / ment dans leur nudité)

—"la critique", dit Tzara / "humour"

Dada systématisé par Tzara

je n'aimais / pas Tzara / finalement, / trop ironique / et un peu / paternaliste / envers moi

Breton réduit le temps de / fabrication mais laisse / trop la place aux retours, / à cause de la main de l'homme et de / ses associations-clichés (mêmes profondes)

nous lettristes, libérons toutes les / particules du mot (y compris celles- / onomatopées, etc, qui battaient

Figure 25. Lettrist page from Maurice Lemaître's *Les Nécrophages de Dada*, 1967. Reproduced from Maurice Lemaître, *le lettrisme devant dada.*

forts of the surrealists. "Surrealism is a big box which dispenses mass-produced prophets. You put in your penny and out comes slather, anathemas, and messages." [20] Isou agrees with Tzara that, contrary to its stated aims, surrealism, "when all's said and done, despite its terrible and furious airs, . . . is still literature and it ends up where it began: at a literary café." [21]

Yet, Isou turns against Tzara, accusing him of letting surrealism erode away the solid achievement of dada. This, as Isou points out, was a blow against linguistic liberty.

> Avec le surréalisme meurt le mythe des mots en liberté. La phrase renaît. Elle redevient l'unité du délire. Avec ses traditions, ses ressources. On réhabilite la période, le balancement des propositions. [22]

> [The myth of words in liberty perishes with surrealism. The sentence is reborn and once again becomes the unity of delirium with its traditions and resources. The complete sentence is rehabilitated as is the careful balancing of clauses.]

Perhaps lettrism's greatest significance is in its insistence on the word as a *thing* and not as a sign. "Car, contrairement à toute la poésie contemporaine qui a apporté des *styles,* la lettrie a apporté *un contenu.* Car la lettrie est une *chose* et non une *réflexion* sur une chose, non *un arrangement des choses.*" [23] [Because unlike all contemporary poetry which has brought us *styles,* lettrism has brought a *substance,* for letttrism is a *thing* and not a *reflection* on a thing nor *an arrangement of things.*] One cannot help speculating about this insistence on the thing itself by such novelists as Michel Butor and Alain Robbe-Grillet. It seems quite possible that Tzara's efforts contributed to a climate which encouraged an interest in *la chose.* This conviction is supported by an announcement of an exhibition at the Galerie J. in Paris of "the new realists," one of whose number is Jean Tinguely. The title of this announcement is "40 degrees (C) above DADA." What the "new realists" propose "is the passionate adventure of the real, perceived *in itself* [my italics] and not through the prism of conceptual or imaginative transcription." [24] These new artists have accepted the dada "readymades" of Marcel Duchamp as the basis of their new expression. The lettrists use "readymade" sounds in essentially the same way. A lettrist definition of poetry bears this out.

> Je la définirais comme re-création *perverse* du monde. Son matériel, le mot, est élevé par elle de sa situation bassement utilitaire à un palier supérieur où, d'un certain point de vue, il se suffit à lui-même. De moyen, d'instrument, de trait d'union entre l'homme et les choses—de substitut des choses—le mot devient lui-même, *presque* la chose. . . . Le mot, cet *instrument,* cette conquête du monde, devenu inutile et bas pour l'art—le lettrisme, poésie de la poésie, le prend *presque* tel quel et l'instaure sur un plan supérieur où il vivra par lui-même, autonome, libéré de ses emplois précédents, remis à *neuf.*[25]

[I would define it as the *perverse* re-creation of the world. The word, its material, is raised up by it from its basely utilitarian situation to a higher level where, from a certain point of view, it is sufficient unto itself. From a means, an instrument, a connecting link between man and things, from a substitute for things, the word itself becomes *almost* the thing. . . . The word, that *instrument,* that conquest of the world, has become useless and base for art. Lettrism, poetry of poetry, takes the word *almost* as is and installs it on a higher level where it exists by itself, autonomous, liberated from its former uses, made *new* again.]

This "almost" quality of the lettrist word is particularly baffling to the reader, although to confound is not specifically the lettrists' intent. Their goal is instead to form a new man not unlike the man the dadaists and surrealists wished to create.

Un homme libéré de sa certitude d'impuissance, libéré des symboles qu'il ne comprenait plus, libéré des tabous qu'il s'était jadis donnés, se conduisant lucidement vers sa plénitude: voilà ce que notre génération par tous les moyens, dont la lettrie, construit.[26]

[What our generation is constructing with all its means, among which figures lettrism, is a man freed from his certitude of impotence, freed from the symbols he no longer understands, freed from the taboos he had formerly given himself, moving lucidly toward his plenitude.]

This wish is essentially the one that Tristan Tzara held from the beginning of dada through the demise of surrealism. He too saw that man had certain self-imposed fetters, and he shared the belief that poetry could help man free himself of those fetters. Has this attempt been successful? Perhaps the inclusion of a typical lettrist poem will illustrate how literary "terrorists" march "lucidly towards plenitude." The reader can judge for himself.

Epithalme

Enn lonn gueuseurs
Lonn gueusalonn
Dours ongueur deurs
Iri-barnn; flonn.

Vol Volomb, omb!
Gliss Kolomb verss
Alk-dar ke derse
Cal ke ri; bomb!

Club, gluk, olirr
Alricaf, ke eruch
Fraicheu, laire
Merdouf altruch!

Rougue erflak
Erraul allmi
Saleul mabour
Etombo Hok!

Envoi
Soussourri, salvani, errestosi galoss!
Slida, blouda, arrka, ourrla,
Ount greechi orrlassi claidon Eross! [27]

This, then, is one of the issues of Tzara's efforts. It is not what he would have desired, and to paraphrase (in lettrist fashion) Picabia's description of cubism, it is probably, after all, a cathedral of "Merdouff."

Figure 26. Tzara at a writers' conference, Palazzo Vecchio, Florence, 1962. Photo Lütfi Ozkök, Sweden.

Conclusion

How important is Tzara, and what is the purport of the
aesthetic theories which he elaborated from 1916 on?
There is no doubt that his life was, like Rimbaud's, "ab-
sorbing, multiple, and indivisible." [1] A part of Tzara's
significance is exemplary. His career parallels that of many
other important writers and painters, such as Pablo Picasso, Paul Eluard, and Louis Aragon. Turning from
youthful individualism and unlimited freedom, he became
a member of that very disciplined group, the communist
party. One explanation for this abdication is furnished by
Albert Camus.

> In that they could not have the best, they still preferred
> the worst. In that respect they were nihilists. . . . The real
> destruction of language which the surrealists so obstinately
> wanted, does not lie in incoherence or automatism. It lies
> in the word *order* . . . and [people like Louis Aragon] . . .

finally found total liberation from morality, even if that liberation coincided with another form of servitude.[2]

Tzara personifies the revolt which finally accepts conformity, and thus he becomes interesting as a case history. He is also extremely important as an interpreter and indeed as a promoter of a poetic schism in this century between what may be called the artists—those who still believe in beauty and in the idea that thought should precede expression, and the descendants of Rimbaud—those who see a new role for poetry. Tzara's dada theory of "words in a hat" showed the way for the surrealists' automatic writing and their fabrication of the *cadavre exquis*. He was a pioneer in this effort to decrease conscious intervention in writing. We examined an outgrowth of this aesthetic that Jean Paulhan calls "terreur" in the preceding chapter. It is an aesthetic which has not escaped strong criticism. Eloquent voices have spoken out against the humiliation of rational content in poetry. Thierry Maulnier has asserted that "les ressources du poète ne sont pas seulement dans la nuit stupéfiée où il élève ses fantômes, elles sont aussi dans le sensible et solide univers où il marche, respire et jouit."[3] [the poet's resources do not exist solely in the stupefying night in which he raises his ghosts. They are also there in the palpable and solid universe where he walks, breathes, and enjoys himself.] Maulnier has also attempted to show that "la matière propre dont dispose le poète n'est pas une *matière mentale*, mais une *matière verbale*." [4] [the proper substance at the poet's disposal is not a *mental substance*, but a *verbal substance*.] Paul Valéry also opposed the confusion of poetry and dream. "The true condition of a true poet is as distinct as possible from the state of dreaming. . . . It is the very one who wants to write down his dream who is obliged to be extremely wide awake." [5] The poet must be fully awake and he must observe poetic conventions, for, as Marcel Raymond says, according to many, "without convention everything collapses, society, man, and his universe, and the poem sinks to the level of stammering." [6] These poets and critics have seen that one of the implications of poetic theories such as those held by Tzara is meaningless stammering. Another implication is art without responsibility. In an art form where the spontaneous is practiced, the artist can disclaim any responsibility with respect to his work. This, of course, can have serious consequences and may indeed be a symptom of an age in which men have lost the courage to make decisions. [7]

Tzara has always maintained that the poet must be a rebel. Is this necessarily true? Must the poet shock the reader, as Tzara counseled in his *sept manifestes DADA* by describing worlds in collision and a coming holocaust? One of the greatest contemporary French poets answers: "No, I cannot write about the apocalypse. I don't believe in the apocalypse." [8] Saint-John Perse is one of the best refutations of Tzara's thesis. His poetry is grave and dignified. It is a poetry that exalts mankind, pointing out man's inherent grandeur and dignity. It is in no way written *against* the reader.

> Behind every manifestation of mobility and fluctuation he [Perse] finds a pure and constant truth, a sign of the immutable. The real world, in the poetry of Perse, becomes *less approximate* [my italics] and less degraded. To man and to every aspiration of man he ascribes some eternal meaning.[9]

Is then the outcome of this study an admission of failure of the revolutionary aims and repeated hopes of Tzara the poet and the critic? It would be well to separate the two Tzaras. It has been pointed out that as a poet he did not meet with unchallenged success either in his attempts to follow his own poetic and linguistic theories or in his desire to become a popular interpreter of the masses' experiences and aspirations, in the communist sense. However, as a critic, Tzara deserves more than contemptuous dismissal. The vigor and continuity of his theories, the variety of his points of view—scientific, Freudian, Jungian, political, historical, linguistic, and artistic—and his role as an incomparable witness of an era prove that Tzara fully deserves the importance he has been given by his fellow poets and critics. His interest in other artists, regardless of the type of school they belonged to, and his sincerity in trying to find a more satisfactory and universal method of communication made of him a humanist, involved deeply and passionately in a poetic solution to the problem of understanding others and the world around us. Tzara grasped the tragedy of human solitude in this century as fully as the existentialists, and (as a critic) he attempted to reach out to others by transcending the restrictions of language and reason. He suggested that man live poetically and communally by sharing the experience of dream and imagination. His entire critical effort must be appreciated as being, in his own words, ". . . a gift to a cause . . . which . . . stirs parallel lives, awakening heavy strata of memory and untranslatable aspirations to as yet scarcely imagined freedoms." [10] Guillaume Apollinaire eloquently expressed the intentions of Tzara and others who fight "always at the frontiers of the limitless and of the future." [11]

> You, whose mouth is made in the image of God,
> A mouth which is order itself,
> Be indulgent when you compare us
> To those who were the perfection of order,
> We who seek adventure everywhere.
>
> We are not your enemies.
> We wish to give ourselves vast strange domains
> Where flowering mystery is offered to him who desires to
>   pluck it.[12]

Notes

Introduction

1. *Surrealist Insurrection* 3 (26 August 1968).
2. *Panorama* (*Chicago Daily News*, 2 November 1968), p. 3.
3. See John Canaday, "Odd Kind of Art," *New York Times,* 27 March 1960, p. x13.
4. See Allen Ginsberg's poem "Howl."
5. "Odd Kind of Art," p. x13.
6. Michel Ragon, *Dubuffet* (New York: Grove Press, 1959).
7. Reported in "Dada Hits West Germany," John Anthony Thwaites, *Arts*, February 1959, pp. 30–37. "The exhibition 'Dada—The Documents of a Movement' was shown at the Kunstverein for the Rhineland and Westphalia in Düsseldorf in September-October 1958, before going on to Frankfort and then to the Stedelijk Museum, Amsterdam."
8. New York: Wittenborn, Schultz, 1951.
9. New York: George Wittenborn, 1958.
10. Paris: Galérie de l'Institut, 1957.
11. *Aires Abstraites* (Geneva: Pierre Cailler, 1957).
12. Paris: Julliard, 1958.

13. Paris: Le Terrain Vague, 1958.

14. Hamburg: Rowohlt, 1964.

15. Paris: Pauvert, 1965.

16. *Etude sur le Théâtre Dada et Surréaliste* (Paris: Gallimard, 1967), p. 12. [My translation. Unless otherwise noted, all translations will be mine.]

17. New York: Grove Press, 1954, pp. 28–29. [Author's translation.]

18. *Situations II* (Paris: Gallimard, 1951), p. 67.

19. *Les Pas Perdus* (Paris: Gallimard, 1924), p. 171.

20. In fact, Mr. Huelsenbeck (now Charles Hulbeck) reiterated this charge at the Spring 1968, Dada-Surrealism Symposium in New York City.

21. A good part of this interesting correspondence is in the private collection of Mr. and Mrs. Leonard Brown, Springfield, Mass.

22. *Les Pas Perdus*, p. 207.

23. *Les Lettres Françaises*, no. 109 (24 mai 1946), p. 4.

24. This first surrealist review ran from December 1924 to December 1929. Pierre Naville and Benjamin Péret were the first directors.

25. André Breton directed this second surrealist review, which ran from July 1930 to May 1933.

26. Paris: Pierre Seghers, 1952.

27. Princeton University Press, 1970.

28. Paris: Bordas, 1947.

29. *Les Lettres Françaises*, no. 1010 (du 2 au 8 janvier 1964), p. 1.

Chapter 1
Dada Manifestoes and Early Celestial Adventures

1. *sept manifestes DADA, lampisteries* (Paris: Jean-Jacques Pauvert, 1963), p. 70. Another recent edition of these

manifestoes is the *Tristan Tzara Sept manifestes Dada* (Paris: Jean-Jacques Pauvert, 1963). This is in the collection "Libertés nouvelles."

2. Attesting this is his *Dada Manifesto 1949* (New York: Wittenborn, Schultz, 1951), and his active participation in the 1968 New York Dada-Surrealism Symposium.

3. Michel Sanouillet, *Dada à Paris* (Paris: Jean-Jacques Pauvert, 1965).

4. *Ibid.*, p. 440.

5. *Les Pas Perdus* (Paris: Gallimard, 1924), p. 124.

6. *Ibid.*, p. 127.

7. *Ibid.*, p. 132.

8. *Ibid.*, p. 136.

9. Zurich: J. Heulberger, 1916. This play was published in a limited edition with woodcuts by Marcel Janco, the first of a number of distinguished artists to collaborate on a book with Tzara. Others include Arp, Picabia, Gris, Miro, Klee, Giacometti, Matisse, Sonia Delaunay, and Marcoussis.

10. Quoted in Robert Motherwell, *The Dada Painters and Poets* (New York: Wittenborn, Schultz, 1951), p. XVX. Ball's book, *Die Flucht aus der Zeit*, was published in Munich by Duncker & Humblot in 1927.

11. Letter of 8 December 1959, from Artists' Village in Tel Aviv.

12. Letter of 3 November 1959 to author.

13. "The Metaphysical Farce: Beckett and Ionesco," *French Review* 32 (February 1959): 319.

14. *La Première Aventure Céleste*. There are no page numbers or division into acts and scenes in this play.

15. This tendency will also be adapted as an integral part of the Lettrist movement. See Chapter VIII.

16. The earth of a city in Taragon?

17. This admiration is expressed in Tzara, "Note sur le Comte

de Lautréamont ou le Cri," *Littérature* (mars 1922), and "Réponse à une enquête" (1922). Both articles are reproduced in *sept manifestes DADA, lampisteries*.

18. Grammatical mistakes abound in Tzara's writings at this time.

19. *Œuvres Poétiques* (Paris: Bibliothèque de la Pléiade, 1959), p. 181.

20. New York: Harcourt, Brace, 1958, p. 266.

21. See "L'Amiral cherche une maison à louer" by Tzara, Janco, and Huelsenbeck, reproduced in *The Dada Painters and Poets*, p. 241.

22. *Nausea*, trans. Lloyd Alexander (New York: New Directions, 1959), p. 172.

23. Originally published in Paris in 1924 by Jean Budry, they have reappeared as *sept manifestes DADA, lampisteries* (Paris: Jean-Jacques Pauvert, 1963). All references will be to the Pauvert edition.

24. *sept manifestes DADA*, p. 15.

25. *Ibid.*, p. 15.

26. *Ibid.*

27. *Ibid.*, p. 16.

28. *La Première Aventure Céleste.*

29. *Esquire*, March 1969, p. 104.

30. *The Dada Painters and Poets*, p. xxv.

31. *sept manifestes DADA*, p. 16.

32. *Les Pas Perdus*, p. 88.

33. *sept manifestes DADA*, p. 19.

34. *Ibid.* pp. 21–22.

35. See Tristan Tzara, *Le Surréalisme et l'Après-Guerre* (Paris: Nagel, 1947).

36. *sept manifestes DADA*, pp. 23–24.

37. *Ibid.*, p. 24.

38. *Ibid.*, pp. 24–25.

39. *Ibid.*, p. 26.
40. Quoted in *Tristan Tzara*, Poètes d'Aujourd'hui (Paris: Seghers, 1952), p. 106.
41. *sept manifestes DADA*, pp. 30–31.
42. *Ibid.*, p. 26.
43. *Ibid.*, p. 33.
44. *Ibid.*, p. 30.
45. *Ibid.*
46. *Ibid.*, p. 34.
47. *Les Manifestes du Surréalisme* (Paris: Le Sagittaire, 1955), p. 24.
48. *Les Pas Perdus*, p. 74. Pierre Prigioni has asserted, however, that from the beginning, Tzara and Breton approached the spontaneous from different angles, Tzara using the spontaneous as a reflection of social reality, and Breton seeing in it "a gratuitousness leading to deeper knowledge of a hidden reality" (*le surréalisme* [Paris: Mouton, 1968], p. 378).
49. *sept manifestes DADA*, p. 34.
50. Translated by Justin O'Brien and published in *From the NRF* (New York: Meridian Books, 1959), p. 14.
51. *sept manifestes DADA*, p. 35.
52. An easier matter for Tzara (who, in Paris, was far removed from his native Rumania) than for his French colleagues.
53. *From the NRF*, p. 15.
54. Reproduced in *The Dada Painters and Poets*, pp. 241–242.
55. *sept manifestes DADA*, p. 38.
56. *Ibid.*, pp. 37, 38.
57. *Ibid.*, p. 45.
58. *Ibid.*, p. 51. Read at the Salle Gaveau in Paris on 22 May 1920. It was published in *391* no. 12, in 1920.
59. *Ibid.*, p. 49.

60. Read at the Galerie Povolozky in Paris on 12 September 1920 and subsequently published in *La Vie des Lettres,* no. 4, 1921.

61. *Ibid.,* p. 58.

62. *Ibid.,* p. 67.

63. *Ibid.,* p. 64.

64. *Modern Language Notes* 73 (June 1958): 434–436.

65. Quoted in Jules Huret, *Enquête sur l'évolution littéraire* (Paris: Bibliothèque Charpentier, 1913), p. 279.

66. Paris: Pierre Seghers, 1945, p. 100. For an amusing account of French critical reaction to Carroll see Philip Thody, "Lewis Carroll and the Surrealists," in *Twentieth Century* 162, no. 975 (May, 1955): 427–434.

67. *The Complete Works of Lewis Carroll* (New York: Random House, 1937), pp. 880–881.

68. *sept manifestes DADA,* p. 68.

69. *Ibid.,* p. 71.

70. The 12 numbers of *291* appeared in New York from 1915–1916.

71. *sept manifestes DADA,* p. 81.

Chapter 2
THE CRITICAL ILLUMINATIONS OF THE *Lampisteries*

1. *sept manifestes DADA, lampisteries* (Paris: Jean-Jacques Pauvert, 1963), p. 106.

2. Paris: Gallimard, 1928.

3. Paris: José Corti, 1930. This discussion of collage lucidly expresses the extra-literary and extra-painterly efforts of dada.

4. Reproduced in Robert Motherwell, *The Dada Painters and Poets* (New York: Wittenborn, Schultz, 1951), pp. 230–231.

5. Willy Verkauf, *Dada, Monograph of a Movement* (New York: George Wittenborn, 1958), p. 173.

6. *Tristan Tzara* (Paris: Seghers, 1952), p. 62.

7. "L'Art Océanien," *A.P.A.M.*, 1951, quoted in *Tzara, Poètes d'Aujourd'hui,"* pp. 64–65.

8. See his articles: "A propos de l'art précolombien," *Les Cahiers d'Art*, No. 4, 1924, and "L'Art et L'Océanie," *Les Cahiers d'Art*, Nos. 2–3, 1929.

9. *lampisteries*, p. 87.

10. *Ibid.*, p. 87.

11. *Ibid.*, p. 87.

12. *Ibid.*, p. 87.

13. *Ibid.*, p. 87.

14. *Ibid.*, p. 87.

15. "The Drunken Boat"

16. *lampisteries*, pp. 87–88.

17. *Ibid.*, p. 88.

18. *Ibid.*, p. 88.

19. *Ibid.*, p. 88.

20. *Ibid.*, p. 88.

21. Paris: Editions du Temps, 1964.

22. Paris: Le Terrain Vague, 1960.

23. Gabrielle Buffet-Picabia, *Aires Abstraites* (Geneva: Pierre Cailler, 1957).

24. *Aires Abstraites*, p. 37.

25. St. Raphaël, 25 February 1922 (one number).

26. Paris, April 1922 (one number).

27. *lampisteries*, p. 112.

28. *Dada, Monograph of a Movement*, p. 58.

29. *lampisteries*, p. 112.

30. Asked by the leftist review, *Commune*, décembre 1933, p. 335.

31. *Ibid.*
32. *Ibid.*
33. *lampisteries*, p. 112.
34. *Ibid.*, p. 113.
35. Text reproduced in *The Dada Painters and Poets*, p. 90.
36. *lampisteries*, pp. 113–114.
37. First published by Figuière, Paris, 1913.
38. *Les Peintres Cubistes* (Geneva: Pierre Cailler, 1950), p. 26.
39. See Anna Balakian, *Surrealism, The Road to the Absolute* (New York: Noonday, 1959), pp. 197–202.
40. Jean Mouton, *Du Silence au Mutisme dans la Peinture* (Paris: Desclée de Brouwer, 1959). See also J. Voellmy, *Aspects du Silence dans la Poésie Moderne* (Zurich, 1952).
41. *lampisteries*, p. 114.
42. Then entry of 30 August 1930 in André Gide's *Journal* is an example.
43. Cited in *Aires Abstraites*, p. 56.
44. *lampisteries*, p. 114.
45. *Ibid.*, pp. 114–115.
46. *Ibid.*, p. 115.
47. *Ibid.*
48. See Jean Paulhan, *Les Fleurs de Tarbes ou La Terreur dans les Lettres* (Paris: Gallimard, 1941).
49. *lampisteries*, p. 103.
50. First published in *Littérature*, mars 1922.
51. *lampisteries*, p. 127.
52. *Ibid.*, pp. 85–86.
53. *Ibid.*, pp. 94–95.
54. "pierre reverdy," published in the *lampisteries*, and in *Dada 3*, December 1917.
55. *lampisteries*, p. 93.

56. *Ibid.*, p. 95.
57. *Ibid.*, p. 100.

Chapter 3
"L'Essai sur la Situation da la Poésie"

1. Paris, Editions GLM, 1946. The second play, *La Deuxième Aventure Céleste*, was published in 1938 by Les Editions des Réverbères in Paris.
2. André Breton, *Les Pas Perdus*, p. 123.
3. *Ibid.*, pp. 130–131.
4. André Breton, *Les Manifestes du Surréalisme* (Paris: Le Saggitaire, 1955).
5. *Ibid.*, p. 27.
6. *Ibid.*, p. 53.
7. *Ibid.*, p. 54.
8. *Ibid.*, p. 84.
9. *Ibid.*
10. *Ibid.*, p. 85.
11. *Tristan Tzara,* Poètes d'Aujourd'hui (Paris: Seghers, 1952), pp. 55–56.
12. *From the NRF* (New York: Meridian Books, 1959), p. 40. [Translated by Justin O'Brien.]
13. *Philosophie du Surréalisme* (Paris: Flammarion, 1955), p. 47.
14. "Essai sur la Situation de la Poésie," p. 15. *LSASDLR* was reprinted by the Arno Press, New York in the Arno Series of Contemporary Art, No. 4.
15. *Alcools* (Garden City, N.Y.: Doubleday & Co., 1964), p. 3. [Translated by William Meredith.]
16. "Essai sur la Situation de la Poésie," pp. 15–16.
17. "The Sun," *Flowers of Evil* (London: Harper & Brothers, 1936), p. 181. [Translated by Edna St. Vincent Millay.]
18. "Essai sur la Situation de la Poésie," p. 15.

19. *The Logic of Hegel* (Oxford: Clarendon Press, 1862), p. 202.

20. *Ibid.*, p. 204.

21. *Psychology of the Unconscious* (New York: Dodd, Mead, 1927), p. 22.

22. *Ibid.*, p. 14.

23. "Essai sur la Situation de la Poésie," p. 19.

24. *Ibid.*, p. 16.

25. *Ibid.*, p. 29.

26. *Ibid.*, p. 30.

27. *Ibid.*, p. 16. The Borel quotation, appearing as an epigraph for his *Rhapsodies* (1833), was taken from a poem by Burger. The lines from Lassailly appeared in his *Les roueries de Trialph, notre contemporain avant son suicide* (1822).

28. *Ibid.*, p. 17.

29. *Ibid.*, p. 20.

30. *Ibid.*

31. *Ibid.*, p. 21.

32. *Ibid.*

33. *Ibid.*, p. 23.

34. "Les Vases Communiquants," *Les Cahiers du Sud* (janvier 1935), p. 64.

35. "Essai sur la Situation de la Poésie," p. 23.

36. Let everyone simply take the trouble to practice poetry." *Les Manifestes du Surréalisme* (Paris: Saggitaire, 1955), p. 35.

37. *Point du Jour* (Paris: Gallimard, 1934), pp. 241–242.

38. Monnerot's article appeared in *Inquisitions*; see Part Three. Eluard's book (*Poésie 42:* Villeneuve-les-Avignon, June 1942), is a collection of poetic excerpts showing that "the authentic poets have never thought that poetry belongs to them exclusively."

39. Paris: Editions Denoël et Steele, 1935.

Chapter 4
Grains et Issues

1. Printed as "Note 1" in *Grains et Issues* (Paris: Editions Denoël et Steele, 1935).
2. *Ibid.*, p. 210.
3. *Ibid.*, p. 211.
4. *Ibid.*
5. André Breton, *Les Manifestes du Surréalisme* (Paris: Le Saggitaire, 1955), p. 28.
6. *Grains et Issues*, p. 213.
7. *Ibid.*, p. 279.
8. *Ibid.*, pp. 281–282.
9. *Ibid.*, p. 282.
10. *Ibid.*
11. *Ibid.*, p. 284.
12. "Grains et Issues," *Les Cahiers du Sud*, mai 1935, p. 496.
13. Gaston Bachelard's "experimental reason" is an application of Tzara's "experimental dream." See Chapter V.
14. Paris: GLM, 1938.
15. One of these social processes was "the revolutionary destiny" of love. However, Tzara leaves commentary on this destiny to other surrealists, such as Breton and Dali, both of whom championed "L'Amour Fou."
16. *Grains et Issues*, pp. 273–274.
17. See Ralph Renwick, Jr., "Dadaism: Semantic Anarchy," *ETC* 15, no. 3 (Spring 1958): 201–209.
18. *Grains et Issues*, p. 275.
19. Victor Hugo, "Réponse à un Acte d'Accusation."
20. *Grains et Issues*, p. 271.
21. *Ibid.*, p. 273.
22. *Ibid.*, pp. 260–261.
23. *Ibid.*, p. 128.

24. *Ibid.*, pp. 128–129.
25. Tzara's poetry is not in the province of this study. He did, however, write five volumes of poetry during this period, and these volumes (*L'Arbre des Voyageurs*, 1930; *L'Homme Approximatif*, 1931; *Où Boivent les Loups*, 1932; *L'Anti-Tête*, 1933; and *Sur le Champ*, 1935) mark him as a productive and significant surrealist poet.
26. Tzara and Breton were, however, reunited in 1960 when they both signed a manifesto directed against the war in Algeria.
27. "Les Poètes dans la Société," *Les Cahiers du Sud*, décembre 1935, pp. 852–856.

Chapter 5
"Initiés et Précurseurs" and *Inquisitions*

1. *Les Cahiers du Sud*, mars 1935, p. 232.
2. *Ibid.*
3. *Commune*, juillet 1935, p. 1202.
4. Tristan Rémy, "Chanson pour le camarade Malva," *Commune*, 1935, pp. 1084–1085.
5. *Commune*, juillet 1935, p. 1230.
6. *Ibid.*, p. 1231.
7. *Minotaure*, 12 décembre 1933, p. 82.
8. *Ibid.*, p. 85.
9. *Ibid.*
10. "Initiés et Précurseurs," *Commune*, juillet 1935, p. 1231.
11. *Ibid.*, p. 1232.
12. *Ibid.*
13. *Ibid.*
14. *Ibid.*, p. 1234.
15. *Ibid.*, p. 1233.
16. *Ibid.*
17. *Ibid.*

18. *Inquisitions,* p. 65.
19. *Ibid.,* p. 42.
20. Pierre Robin, "Les Conférences Dali," *Inquisitions,* p. 51. Roger Caillois expresses this rejection of surrealism differently in an article entitled "Pour une Orthodoxie Militante: Les Tâches Immédiates de la Pensée Moderne." He describes surrealism's failures by saying that its attempt to liberate men's minds had fallen into ". . . half-aesthetic activities which finally take on an insane and purely ritual character." *Inquisitions,* p. 7.
21. *Ibid.,* pp. 1–2.
22. John Cage, who has been called a neo-dadaist composer, has titled one of his albums of electronic music, "Indeterminacy." The sounds seem to be quite free of any pre-determined scheme. The album is Folkways Records, FT 3704.
23. *Inquisitions,* p. 29.
24. One of the aforementioned critics, Jules Monnerot, shows that he agrees with this belief by the title of his contribution to *Inquisitions,* "Remarques sur le rapport de la poésie comme genre à la poésie comme fonction."
25. *Inquisitions,* p. 31.
26. *Ibid.*
27. *Ibid.,* p. 34.
28. The poet, Petrus Borel, called himself "Le Lycanthrope." He apparently felt that he exemplified the saying "Man is a wolf to man."
29. *Inquisitions,* p. 47.
30. *Ibid.*
31. "Il Secolo," Interview of Paul Claudel, printed in *Comoedia,* 17 June 1925.
32. Paris, 1 juillet 1925.
33. *Inquisitions,* p. 47.

34. *Ibid.,* p. 48.

35. *Ibid.* Valéry and Cocteau are disposed of quickly and unsympathetically. It should be noted, however, that the surrealists paid an unwilling compliment to Valéry by parodying several of his remarks. Valéry's "A poem must be an Intellectual feast" was changed by Breton and Eluard to "A poem must be an intellectual debacle." The fact that the word "intellectual" is no longer capitalized is obviously significant.

36. Tzara went to Spain in the late thirties and at the Second International Writers Conference in Valencia on July 10, 1937, he gave an important speech on "The Individual and the Conscience of the Writer," warning that "the writer, if he doesn't wish to disappear as such, must take a [political] stand." After the fall of France ". . . he experienced all the refuges. Some thought they were discovering a great unknown poet named T. Tristan in our clandestine or contraband reviews. History will retain the role and influence of Tzara who was, during those four years in all the struggles, with the National Writers Committee. . . ." René Lacôte, *Tristan Tzara,* Poètes d'Aujourd'hui (Paris: Seghers, 1952), p. 59.

Chapter 6
CRITICAL PERSPECTIVES

1. Preface for: Henri Rousseau, *Une Visite à l'Exposition de 1899* (Geneva: Pierre Cailler, 1947).

2. Preface for Tristan Corbière, *Les Amours Jaunes* (Paris: Le Club Français du Livre, 1950).

3. Introduction to *Picasso* (Geneva: Albert Skira, 1948).

4. Introduction to *Les Œuvres Complètes de Rimbaud* (Lausanne: Editions Grand-Chêne, 1948).

5. Introduction to François Villon, *Poésies* (Paris: Audin, 1949).

6. "René Crevel," *Les Etoiles* (18 septembre 1945).

7. "De la Solitude des images chez Pierre Reverdy," *Le Point* (juillet 1946).

8. "Paul Eluard et les images fraternelles," *Les Lettres Françaises* (novembre 1955).

9. Guillaume Apollinaire, *Alcools*, Premières épreuves commentées et annotées par Tristan Tzara (Paris: Le Club du Meilleur Livre, 1953).

10. *Une Visite à l'Exposition*, p. 1.

11. *Ibid.*

12. *Ibid.*, p. 2.

13. *Ibid.*, p. 12.

14. *Inquisitions*, p. 67.

15. Paris: Galerie Simon, 1925.

16. *Une Visite à l'Exposition*, p. 14.

17. Roger Shattuck, *The Banquet Years* (New York: Harcourt, Brace, 1958), p. 86.

18. *Une Visite à l'Exposition*, p. 16.

19. *Ibid.*, p. 17.

20. *Ibid.*

21. *Les Cahiers d'Art* 37: 195–196.

22. *Ibid.*, p. 195.

23. *Les sept manifestes DADA, The Dada Painters and Poets*, p. 78.

24. *Une Visite à l'Exposition*, p. 25.

25. *Les Cahiers d'Art* 37: 196.

26. *Une Visite à l'Exposition*, p. 34.

27. Tristan Corbière, *Les Amours Jaunes* (Paris: Le Club Français du Livre, 1950).

28. Tristan Tzara, "Tristan Corbière ou les Limites du Cri," *Europe*, no. 60 (décembre 1950): 87–96.

29. Albert Sonnenfeld, *L'Œuvre Poétique de Tristan Corbière* (Paris: Presses Universitaires de France, 1960), p. 156.

30. "Tristan Corbière ou les Limites du Cri," p. 87.

31. *Ibid.*

32. *Ibid.*

33. This is probably also true for Tzara. Indeed, René Lacôte said that Tzara attempted to express "à l'infini" his personality and found absolute solitude as a result. *Tristan Tzara*, Les Poètes d'Aujourd'hui (Paris: Seghers, 1952), p. 77.

34. "Tristan Corbière ou les Limites du Cri," p. 88.

35. *Ibid.*, p. 88. Jean Rousselot, writing after Tzara, repeats this idea, saying: ". . . et le mot 'peindre' est celui qui définit le mieux l'art de Corbière." *Tristan Corbière*, Poètes d'Aujourd'hui (Paris: Seghers, 1951), p. 36. Rousselot pays tribute to Tzara's article particularly with respect to the mention of "verbal exasperation," and he remarks that Corbière's tone is not unlike that of Rutebeuf and Villon.

36. *Tristan Corbière*, Poètes d'Aujourd'hui, p. 82.

37. André Breton, *Anthologie de l'Humour Noir* (Paris: Seghers, 1940).

38. "Tristan Corbière ou les Limites du Cri," p. 91.

39. *Ibid.*, p. 92.

40. *Ibid.*

41. *Ibid.*, p. 93.

42. *Ibid.*

43. *Picasso*, Les Trésors de la Peinture Française (Geneva: Skira, 1948).

44. *Documents Surréalistes*, p. 277.

45. "Picasso et les Chemins de la Connaissance," no pagination.

46. *Ibid.*

47. *Ibid.*
48. Zurich: Collection Dada, 1918.
49. Cf. *Midis Gagnés* (Paris: Editions Denoël, 1948).
50. "Picasso et les Chemins de la Connaissance."
51. *Ibid.*
52. Leonard B. Meyer, "Art by Accident," *Horizon* (September 1960), p. 121.
53. "L'Unité de Rimbaud," *Europe,* no. 36 (décembre 1948), pp. 25–34. Rimbaud, *Les Œuvres Complètes,* Introduction par Tristan Tzara (Lausanne: Editions Grand-Chêne, 1948).
54. For an excellent discussion of this aspect of Rimbaud's career see Frederic St. Aubyn, "The Social Consciousness of Rimbaud," *Yale French Studies* 2, no. 2, pp. 26–33. For a study of myths concerning Rimbaud see Etiemble, *Le Mythe de Rimbaud* (Paris: Gallimard, 1952).
55. "Matin," *Une Saison en Enfer,* trans. William M. Davis in *An Anthology of French Poetry from Nerval to Valéry in English Translation* (Garden City: Doubleday Anchor Books, 1958), p. 129.
56. Henry Bouillane de Lacoste's thesis, *Rimbaud et le problème des Illuminations* (Paris: Mercure de France, 1940), which suggests that *Les Illuminations* postdate *Une Saison en Enfer* would, of course, if accepted, invalidate part of Tzara's theory on Rimbaud.
57. "L'Unité de Rimbaud," p. 25.
58. *Ibid.*
59. *Ibid.*, p. 27.
60. *Ibid.*
61. *Ibid.*, p. 31.
62. *La Symbolique de Rimbaud* (Paris: Vieux Colombier, 1947).
63. "L'Unité de Rimbaud," p. 27.

64. *Ibid.*, p. 28.
65. *Ibid.*, p. 29.
66. *Ibid.*, p. 33.
67. See Albert Camus, *The Rebel* (New York: Alfred A. Knopf, 1967).
68. *Ibid.*, p. 89 [translated by Anthony Bower].
69. "De la solitude des images chez Pierre Reverdy," *Le Point* (juillet 1946).
70. "Paul Eluard et les images fraternelles."
71. Commentary and annotation of Guillaume Apollinaire, *Alcools.*
72. "René Crevel," *Les Etoiles* (18 septembre 1945).
73. Introduction to François Villon, *Poésies.*
74. *Alcools*, p. 4.
75. "Paul Eluard et les images fraternelles," p. 1.
76. *Ibid.*
77. "De la solitude des images chez Pierre Reverdy," p. 1.
78. "René Crevel," p. 1.

Chapter 7
Le Surréalisme et l'Après-Guerre

1. Paris: Nagel, 1947.
2. *Le Surréalisme et l'Après-Guerre*, p. 17.
3. For an analysis of this see Paul-Louis Faye, "Dada and the Temper of 1917," *University of Colorado Studies* 1, no. 4 (October 1941). Also see Bentley B. Gilbert and Paul P. Bernard, "The French Army Mutinies of 1917," *The Historian* 22, no. 1 (November 1959): 24–41.
4. *Dada, Monograph of a Movement* (New York: George Wittenborn, 1958), p. 29.
5. *Ibid.*, p. 109.
6. *Le Surréalisme et l'Après-Guerre*, p. 50.
7. *Ibid.*

8. Quoted in Robert Motherwell, *The Dada Painters and Poets* (New York: Wittenborn, Schultz, 1951), p. 51.

9. *Le Surréalisme et l'Après-Guerre*, p. 51. His argument seems a little specious. This postwar interpretation of dada cannot be accepted as accurate and objective. One must return to *les sept manifestes DADA* for a real comprehension of the aims of dada.

10. *Ibid.*, p. 21.

11. *Ibid.*, p. 8.

12. Tristan Tzara, *Midis Gagnés* (Paris: Editions Denoël, 1939), p. 95.

13. *Le Surréalisme et l'Après-Guerre*, p. 9.

14. *Ibid.*, p. 74.

15. *Ibid.*, p. 30.

16. Paul Eluard, *Capitale de la Douleur*, "L'Amoureuse."

17. *Le Surréalisme et l'Après-Guerre*, pp. 40–41.

18. *Ibid.*

19. Anna Balakian remarks that "Aragon's verse has the epic tone of Hugo; and Eluard's simplicity, which with the surrealist perspective had a ubiquitous elusiveness, becomes in these posthumously published poems limpingly prosaic and monotonously evangelical in cadence." *Surrealism, the Road to the Absolute* (New York: Noonday Press, 1959), p. 183.

20. *Le Surréalisme et l'Après-Guerre*, p. 41.

21. See C. G. Christofides, "Gaston Bachelard's Phenomenology of the Imagination," *Romanic Review* 52, no. 1 (February 1961): 36–47.

22. *Le Surréalisme et l'Après-Guerre*, p. 57.

23. *Ibid.*

24. Gaston Bachelard, *L'Air et les Songes* (Paris: José Corti, 1943), p. 14.

25. Otto Rank, *Beyond Psychology* (New York: Dover, 1958), p. 14.

26. *Le Surréalisme et l'Après-Guerre*, p. 61.

27. *Ibid.*, p. 68. Tzara's most complete study of the relationship between political and linguistic revolution is, of course, found in *Grains et Issues*.

Chapter 8
LETTRISM

1. Maurice Lemaître, *le lettrisme devant dada* (Paris: Centre de Créativité, 1967), p. 17.

2. Quoted in Robert Motherwell, *The Dada Painters and Poets* (New York: Wittenborn, Schultz, 1951), p. 26.

3. *Ibid.*, p. xix.

4. *Ibid.*

5. *Ibid.*, p. xx.

6. *Ibid.*, pp. 129–130.

7. Zurich: Collection Dada, 1918.

8. It is remarkable how much the intransigence and passion of Isou bring to mind the Tzara of the dada period. There are personal resemblances also. Isou was born Isidore Goldstein in Rumania. He founded lettrism in Paris at the age of twenty-one. Tzara, also of Jewish descent, was twenty-three when he came to Paris to promote dada.

9. *Fontaine*, no. 62 (octobre 1947).

10. *Fontaine*, p. 530.

11. *Ibid.*

12. *Ibid.*

13. *Ibid.*

14. *Ibid.*, p. 531.

15. *Ibid.*, p. 532.

16. *Ibid.* If *poetry* is soft and unchallenging for the lettrists,

Isou personally, in his attacks on other poets, reminds one of some of the more violent dadaists, such as Arthur Cravan. Aragon, who was unpleasant enough himself as a young man, gets his comeuppance from Isou. "Because the patriot Aragon has slept with a camp-follower Elsa (whom he takes the liberty of comparing with France) and because he accompanied that sad act (the bedding-down) with a worthless poem ("Elsa's Waltz"), here he is now aspiring to the title of National Bard." *Fontaine*, p. 543.

17. *Ibid.*, p. 544.
18. *Ibid.*, pp. 544–545.
19. *Ibid.*, p. 545. It is to be noticed that Tzara could well be included in this criticism. Of course, it depends on the interpretation of the word "dreams."
20. *Ibid.*
21. *Ibid.*
22. *Ibid.*, p. 547.
23. *Ibid.*, p. 550.
24. Pierre Restany, "A 40° au-dessus de DADA," Galerie J., du 17 mai au 10 juin 1961.
25. André Lambaire, "Considérations sur une Phonétique Lettriste," *Fontaine*, no. 62 (octobre 1947): 552–553.
26. *Ibid.*, p. 553.
27. Clement Swenssen, "Epithalame," *Fontaine*, p. 565.

CONCLUSION

1. See Chapter VI, p. 176.
2. Albert Camus, *The Rebel* (New York: Alfred A. Knopf, 1967), pp. 94–95.
3. Thierry Maulnier, *Introduction à la Poésie Française* (Paris: Gallimard, 1939), p. 17.
4. *Ibid.*, p. 21.

5. Paul Valéry, *The Art of Poetry* (New York: Pantheon Books, 1958), p. 11.

6. Marcel Raymond, *From Baudelaire to Surrealism* (New York: Wittenborn, Schultz, 1950), p. 344.

7. See Leonard B. Meyer, "Art by Accident," *Horizon* (September 1960). Also see Roger Maren, "The Musical Numbers Game," *The Reporter* (6 March 1958).

8. Quoted by Guillaume Hanoteau in "Monsieur Saint-John Perse, vous avez le Nobel," *Paris Match* (5 novembre 1960), p. 102.

9. Wallace Fowlie, *Mid-Century French Poets* (New York: Grove Press, 1955), pp. 94–95.

10. "Tristan Corbière ou les Limites du Cri," *Europe,* no. 60 (décembre 1950): p. 87; see Chapter VI, p. 160.

11. Guillaume Apollinaire, "La Jolie Rousse."

12. *Ibid.*

Index

Note on the Author

Elmer Peterson, born in Albert Lea, Minnesota, in 1930, is professor and chairman of romance languages at Colorado College in Colorado Springs. He received his B.A. degree from Carleton College in 1952, his M.A. degree from Middlebury College in 1957, and his Ph.D. from Colorado University in 1962. Following his graduation from Carleton he served three years in the Navy as an air intelligence officer in the Far East. His extensive researches in French and European literature have taken him to Europe many times, and he met Tristan Tzara in Paris in 1962. He was director of the Colorado University-Kansas University Study Center at Bordeaux in 1965–66. He has lectured extensively on such subjects as "The University in France," "Dadaism," and "Surrealism."

The text of this book was set in Garamond Linotype and printed by Offset on Warren's Olde Style Wove manufactured by S. D. Warren Company, Boston, Mass. Composed, printed and bound by Quinn & Boden Company, Inc., Rahway, N.J.

"... the dada spirit is alive and well today. The world is once again, as it was in 1916, thrust into a climate of doubt and hopelessness. ... Coupled with this crisis of the mind is an acute linguistic crisis ... a modern breakdown in communication." Thus Elmer Peterson begins this timely analysis of the major French poet and critic, Tristan Tzara. While his prime concern is a detailed consideration of Tzara's works and theories, the author also draws a clear parallel between the antics and aims of the dada and surrealist movements (and their successors) and the present-day cultural upheavals both in this country and abroad. As an example, graffiti from the Paris student strike of 1968 are used as epigraphs throughout the book with astonishing, sometimes shocking, aptness.